Ghostly Tales

OF SELECTED

VIRGINIA

STATE PARKS

T0161794

by P.M. Elton

Adventure Publications, Inc.

"Each living person in all God's universe is a radiating center of the same perfect One, some radiating more and some less, according to the awakened consciousness of the individual."

— H. Emilie Cady, 1894

DEDICATION

This book is dedicated to all the tireless Virginia State Park staff who make our Commonwealth a jewel to behold and one that allowed me to raise my two sons, Alexander (AJ) and Lance, in an environment rich beyond measure.

PHOTO CREDITS

Pg. 52 Occoneechee Plantation, Courtesy Virginia State Parks; **Pg. 60** Mount Bleak House, Courtesy Tonya L. Hishchynsky; **Pg. 64** Fort, Courtesy Harold Jerrell; **Pg. 66** Karlan Mansion, Caylor Depot, Indian Creek, Courtesy Mike Brindle

10 9 8 7 6 5 4 3 2 1

Copyright 2015 by P.M. Elton
Published by Adventure Publications, Inc.
820 Cleveland Street South
Cambridge, MN 55008
1-800-678-7006
www.adventurepublications.net
Printed in the U.S.A.

ISBN: 978-1-59193-483-7

TABLE OF CONTENTS

ACKNOWLEDGMENTS

These legends and lore are the compilation of many shared tales, including those with a smidgen of misinformation. I have taken hints and ideas and have expounded on them, sincerely believing that there was more to tell than that which rose from the informant's lips. On the other hand, there are ghost stories within these pages, I am positive, that are woefully understated, especially at Chippokes Plantation State Park. But given that the majority of Virginia's state parks were built on or near historically significant grounds, it is apparent to some that most of the properties exhibit a unique energy that can enliven the park experience, whether you're a visitor, volunteer or employee. There were also occasions while traveling the back roads of Virginia when local folks shared stories about nearby places known to exhibit paranormal activity. Then there were other individuals who may not have had a ghostly tale to share but certainly provided useful historical data. Much appreciation is also extended to the park personnel, who took their valuable time to escort me directly to pertinent, and very possibly haunted, locations within the parks.

Appreciation is extended in particular to one "Friends of the Park" group: the Friends of Chippokes State Park. Thanks are also due to the following individuals: Nathan Younger, Shirley Roberg, Kathryn Lane, Danette Poole, George Lee Dowdy, Laura Moss, John and Judy Taminger, Jim Kelly, Tom Cervanak, Sarah Lankford, Diane Lanier, Jon Tustin, John Gresham, Lee Wilcox, Chris Calkins, Robert Chapman, Nancy Horton, Maranda Maness, Megan Krager, Charlie Conner, Johnny and Jo Finch, Lauri Schular, Budd Reitnauer, Sharon Ewing, Mike Brindle, Tim Skinner, Tonya

L. Hishchynsky, Scott Shanklin, Craig and Karen Seaver, and posthumously, to Mark Hufeisen.

Additionally, I would like to thank my husband's very talented and dedicated executive assistant, Paula Hill. She was my Richmond editor, my confidant, the person who always made me laugh, and most important, my friend.

Lastly, I could not have accomplished such a feat without the encouragement, delicate criticism, and rich historical knowledge of my husband, Joe Elton. I will forever be thankful for so much!

INTRODUCTION

At one time or another, most folks have imagined spending a night in a haunted house. At Virginia's state parks, you can. Its parks offer a number of "haunted" locations where you can stay, all while enjoying some of the best scenery the Commonwealth has to offer.

Ghosts of Virginia State Parks—what a silly subject. Interesting, and popular for sure, but why? Having had the pleasure of exploring each of Virginia's state parks on multiple occasions, I am familiar with the exemplary lands and people who make up this dynamic system. My senses have frequently reached overload during some park visits, and I've experienced some truly eerie and unworldly things on some visits. Without question, I firmly believe that ghosts are present in Virginia's state parks.

With that said, I've always been in tune with the calmer, less frightening side of paranormal activity. If you're hoping for a litany of horror tales, this book is not for you. But weird, inexplicable, and somewhat spooky happenings abound in park after park within these pages.

In my own life, I've long experienced run-ins with the unknown and mysterious. One such phenomenon lasted beyond a brief moment and involved what I believe was a face-to-face encounter with a ghost. The incident happened at my parents' small farm outside Columbus, Ohio, in the late 1970s. There was something peculiar and uneasy about the house, and on occasion, it sent me into a state of chilly fright. It was here that I grew keenly aware of the paranormal. And it just so happened this was my residence when the popular 1973 movie *The Exorcist* hit the big screen.

The film was a very dark awakening for me. Not growing up in a Christian household, I knew nothing about the supernatural wonders and gifts of our Creator and how to defend myself spiritually from demonic influences. I was a ripe victim for the snares of Satan, whom I believe immensely enjoyed his Hollywood portrayal.

The very evening I saw the movie I retired to bed a bit scared and shaken, but refusing to replay in my mind the hellish sights and sounds, I comfortably drifted off to sleep. I hadn't been asleep long when all of a sudden I was awakened by sounds of thumping in the attic. The noise was directly above my bedroom. I sat up straight and the noise ceased. Laying my head back down, the thumping promptly began again. This time it sounded like it was bouncing from one rafter to the next. Scared out of my wits, I dashed into the family room where my parents were seated and asked them about the noise. They looked at me in bewilderment, then looked at each other, then back at me as if I had lost all reasoning. I retreated back to the bedroom and the noise started up again. Refusing to give the noise acknowledgment, eventually I fell asleep and was relieved when daybreak came and all was quiet above my head.

It was only a matter of a few days after this mystifying racket that my mother started noticing a foul smell in the kitchen. She examined every crack and crevice, but she never could identify the origin of the putrid stench. My father and I both noticed the unsettling odor as well but neither of us could find its cause. Over the course of several months of battling the smell, my parents decided the best course of action was to replace the carpet, replace the curtains, and to paint the cabinets inside and out. Despite all this, the bad smell remained. It was only later in life, when I stumbled on writings about how ghosts and spirits attach themselves to one or more of our senses, that I recalled the peculiar kitchen problem in my parents' home. According to paranormal experts, odors are one of the most common indicators of a ghostly presence or manifestation. Skeptics reason that unusual smells are nothing more than scents trapped in a material substance, such as fabric or wood, which are then released when atmospheric changes occur. Nevertheless, after my parents' feeble attempt to cleanse the kitchen, the foul odor was persistent, leading me to believe it was the phantom odor of a haunting.

With the combination of the mysterious sounds in the attic and the kitchen stench fresh in our minds, my father and I began hearing car doors slam in our driveway. The house sat far from other houses, and the slamming doors sounded like they were just outside the family room window. I ignored the sound, believing things wouldn't get worse if I paid them no mind.

My actual encounter with the apparition occurred at the onset of a weekend. Friday nights were my parents' evening out. My father zoomed home from downtown Columbus after a long week's work, picked up my schoolteacher mother and they both headed back into Columbus for an evening of dining and relaxing. With parents out of the way, I was set to enjoy my evening as well. After sports practice that evening, I hustled down the backcountry roads in my red, shiny VW Beetle. Home at last, I hurried through the chore list my mother always left behind, grabbed my purse and headed out the door. My parents' home was an attractive yellow ranch poised beautifully on a curve, perfect for the passerby to admire as they rounded the bend. In my hurried state, I quickly closed the front door behind me and turned to bolt down the blocky cinnamon path toward the scarlet Beetle. That's when I saw it—or him. He was a trim man in his late 20s or early 30s and was casually leaning against the driver's side fender and smiling at me. Taken aback, I froze as I stared in astonishment. It wasn't the young man that scared me; it was the fact that I could see directly through him. My body clutched with fear; I was seeing a transparent entity. Seconds ticked by, but I made myself focus enough to confirm that it was truly my VW fender that was visible through his misty image. My entire body began to shake, but I managed to gain control of my clattering assortment of keys, and with quivering hands, I unlocked the front door. The door thrust inward and I bounded into the entryway in one fell swoop. Slamming the door, I stood silent, my heart pounding. Eventually, I mustered up enough courage and reopened the door. As I peeked out to the driveway, I could see he was still there. *Oh God,* I thought! Now what? My facial expression must have been comical, because his smile turned to laughter. The strange thing was that the laughter was not audible, but from his expression, it was clear he was laughing, because he tossed his head back as if enjoying a hearty belly laugh. Then, he turned sideways and evaporated.

Now if I heard that story, even today, I'd doubt the storyteller, but it really happened to me, and it forever changed my life. Years passed before I told a soul, but eventually, I told friends, and eventually I married and started my own family and I didn't think much about that day again until I resided in Virginia for a few years. It was then that my mother and father informed me of their plans to move from the farm. When the real estate inspector went through the house, he informed them about numerous burned roof joists. Questions remain in my mind about that house. Why weren't they informed about the burned joists when they bought the home? Why did the attic noise eventually cease? Why did the kitchen odor remain, and from where did the driveway sounds emerge? Was it because this spirit was not an evil apparition but one that just desired to communicate? Who was that mysterious transparent man and where did he come from? Was he a victim of the previously unknown house fire? Oddly, in all the years my parents resided at that home, not one neighbor ever mentioned a house fire, nor did the property deed. If I'm honest, I've never quite gotten over what I saw that day.

I wrote this book for two reasons. First, to bring together real-life stories of extraordinary occurrences within state parks from all over the Commonwealth. Second, for you to enjoy, and in the hopes that it helps the reader open their eyes to the mysterious and wonderful. (Or as E.B. White put it, "Always be open to wonder.")

Over the years I have come to realize that each park is like a small village or town. Roads, trails, cabins, campgrounds, picnic areas, restaurants, public swimming beaches and pools, water and waste system, law enforcement, gift shops and camp stores—they have it all. (And almost every park has one or more cemeteries.) What's more, the staff wear many hats and they are professionally trained and routinely provide customer service excellence. They are places people go to have a good time.

They are also places where strange things have—and do—happen. It is my goal to give you a taste of the scenery and settings, the peoples and places at each park, along with supernatural tales to share around the campfire. So get out there and discover (or rediscover) the wonders Virginia State Parks have to offer.

FOREWORD

State parks give us all an ownership stake in the American dream. They enhance our lives and our love of country. They are places we go to off-load the daily tension of life and seek a tonic for the mind, body and spirit.

Virginia's state parks were imagined during the Roaring Twenties, birthed during the Great Depression and have grown to keep pace with the Commonwealth's remarkable growth in population. According to current scientific analysis, they are places that have supported native cultures for nearly 15,000 years—and perhaps longer. They showcase the rich natural and cultural resources of a place called home by many of our founding fathers.

Virginia's parks provide outdoor recreation venues in some of the region's and country's most remarkable landscapes. Parks on the Atlantic Ocean and the Chesapeake Bay highlight marine life, maritime forests and sand dune habitats, as well as salt marshes and big open water for boating, fishing and sailing. Our parks on some of America's great rivers (including the Potomac, Rappahannock, York, James, Shenandoah and New) provide spectacular scenery, great floating and fishing opportunities and trails with incomparable scenic views.

The central Piedmont section of the state is where the mountains and coastal plain connect and the geography is both diverse and breathtakingly beautiful. It's also where much of the Civil War was fought, including the best part … the end. And lastly, state parks in Virginia's historic Appalachian Mountains give visitors opportunities to hike, bike, horseback ride and enjoy immersion in nature in the world-famous Shenandoah and Blue Ridge Mountains and our majestic Allegheny Highlands.

Beginning in 1607, Virginia was the first area visited and permanently settled by English colonists, and it played a central role in the American Revolution that created our nation and the Civil War that kept it together. Enjoying the great outdoors and learning about America's cultural heritage is central to the state park experience. From the beginning, it was determined that our state parks should be places where people could find a therapeutic tonic for the mind, body and spirit. They were also viewed as places where the "real Virginia" and our native flora and fauna would be conserved for future generations to see and study. And, in the beginning it was believed that if proper facilities were constructed to serve modern park visitors—cabins, campgrounds, picnic and swimming areas, visitor centers and most importantly a great network of trails—our parks would be healthy places for people to recreate, and they would stimulate outdoor recreation and tourism that is so important for a healthy economy.

After more than 80 years, it is clear that those who dreamed and built our state parks have realized virtually everything they imagined. From 90,000 visits in 1936 to 9 million in 2014, it is obvious that our parks remain important to citizens. Those 9 million visitors had an economic impact on the state of more than $220 million. And with each visit, a person leaves feeling refreshed, reinvigorated and healthier.

This particular book is written by my best friend of nearly 40 years. She has traveled the state with me since 1994, visiting state parks. She has been affectionately referred to as the First Lady of Virginia State Parks. Patricia is more sensitive and tuned in to all the dimensions our world—

and others—have to offer. She has read and studied the paranormal experiences of others, had some of her own and has been intrigued with things spiritual and mystical her entire life. As we have traveled throughout Virginia's state parks, she has gathered stories and listened to firsthand accounts of people whose lives have been touched in mysterious ways.

She has been encouraged for years to share what she has learned. This book, which has been talked about for many years, represents her first foray in telling ghost stories. It represents about one-third of Virginia's state parks, but geographically represents the width and depth of Virginia. In future volumes, she proposes to share what she has heard from the other state parks, along with those new stories that come her way about the parks covered in this edition.

We imagine that once more people know she is chronicling the ghosts of Virginia State Parks, many more stories will come out of the woodwork.

It's indeed a brave person who is willing to talk about things some don't think even exist. It is even braver to work with one's spouse on a project of mutual interest. It certainly has been a learning and growing experience for us.

My recommendation is to fix yourself a spot of tea or coffee, or perhaps a glass of wine, settle into a nice easy chair and let your imagination and senses take you on a journey—to places near or far and dimensions wherever they may exist. Enjoy the journey and long live our parks and the USA!

Joe Elton
State Parks Director (1994–2014)

Bear Creek Lake State Park

CHARLES IRVING THORNTON
TOMBSTONE
has been registered as a
**Virginia
Historic
Landmark** ▶
pursuant to the authority vested in the
Virginia Historic Landmarks Commission
Act of 1966

PARK OVERVIEW

ACRES: 326   **FOUNDED:** July 1939

NEARBY: Jesse Thomas historical marker and Charles Irving Thornton tombstone; High Bridge Trail State Park, Lee's Retreat Driving Tour

NOTABLE VISITORS: George Washington, General Lafayette, Thomas Jefferson, Patrick Henry, John Randolph, Colonel John Chiswell and Charles Dickens

ABOUT THE PARK

Buried in the heart of Virginia's Piedmont in the midst of the 16,242-acre oak-hickory and loblolly state forest is Bear Creek Lake State Park, which boasts all the amenities of larger parks but not the crowds. It is a traditional destination state park and includes thirteen well-appointed housekeeping cabins with all the comforts of home.

The park's swimming beach and hiking, fishing and paddling opportunities provides most of the recreation for visitors. A meeting and reception hall provides a scenic venue for local businesses, family gatherings and weddings.

PARK HISTORY

Quiet, But with a Most Unusual History

Located between Richmond and Farmville, Cumberland County is a rural and scenic place often seen in passing, either on the drive to Richmond or on a trip to Charlottesville or Roanoke.

It's this central location that has ensured that Cumberland County has enjoyed many famous visitors through the centuries. The list includes Washington and Lafayette and virtually every Governor of Virginia, not to mention Thomas Jefferson, who designed the County Courthouse.

Settlement of the county dates to as early as 1723, when the first recorded claim was filed on 2,870 acres on Willis Creek. Along the main roads, taverns providing food, lodging and provisions for travelers became the center of community life. One notable example was the Effingham Tavern, which was located across from the Cumberland Courthouse and named for a colonial governor of the same name. On April 22, 1776, Carter Henry Harrison read one of the first calls for independence at the tavern. John Mayo and William Fleming presented this statement to the Virginia Convention. Their call led Thomas Jefferson to draft the Declaration of Independence. Other notable guests in the tavern were Patrick Henry, John Randolph and Colonel John Chiswell, an enthusiastic explorer and the first European to discover Southwest Virginia's lead deposits. One of Chiswell's brief stops in Cumberland ended on a sordid note.

The year was 1756 and Chiswell was westward bound. He had partnered with two men in a mining operation. They were William Byrd III, the head of Virginia's Byrd dynasty, and John Robinson, the Speaker of the House of Burgess and the Treasurer of Virginia. Each had contributed a third of the funds and an equal number of slaves toward their new mining prospect in the mountains. Author James Tucker details what happened next in his book, *John Chiswell of the Southwest Virginia Frontier*: "...easily distracted, William Byrd III attended to social amusements elsewhere" while all the while Robinson skimmed money out of the Colony's funds. In a huff, Chiswell headed southwest, stopping in Cumberland County for a short respite. Tucker describes Chiswell as "distraught and angry" upon entering Mosby's Tavern. Dousing his anger with a few too many libations, Chiswell got in a heated discussion with Robert Rutledge about loyalty to the throne of England. Rutledge was a fiery Scot who found Chiswell's words contemptible and threw a glass of wine in the loyalist's face. The Colonel was enraged and swiftly drew his sword without further thought, ruthlessly stabbing Rutledge to death. Tucker quotes the reported words of Chiswell, "I aimed for his heart and I found it. He's dead and I killed him. He deserved it, damn him."

Being a well-connected individual, Chiswell was later exonerated; this left the townfolk in disgust over the injustice that had occurred on their soil. When Chiswell reached Williamsburg he found that reports of his horrible deed had followed him. Pressure mounted to the point that Colonel Chiswell ended his life with a single shot to the head.

The American Revolution in Cumberland

Other visitors to Bear Creek come to explore a Revolutionary War legend. Located just off a local forest road, there is a historical marker commemorating the Willis River homestead of Colonel Jesse Thomas, who was wounded in the war. According to writer Bessie Thompson Jackson, Colonel Thomas was a "FFV" (First Family of Virginia); Jesse's father was among the first immigrants to the New World in the 1700s. According to records from 1740, his father, Job, was married to Elizabeth, and they

had two teenage sons, Jesse and Phineas, and the family was "well established in Cumberland Co., Va." The young man, Jesse, made frequent trips to England, where he married Sarah Wood of London, but she died within several years. Soon thereafter Jesse found a second bride in nearby Buckingham County. Even though she was 20 years his junior, their marriage resulted in a full household of 12 children who lived comfortably on his extensive plantation.

Why is such a prominent plaque placed on the side of a long lonesome forest road? Well, the Revolutionary War was underway and June 2, 1781, proved to be a fateful night for Jesse, who was home recuperating from a wound incurred at the Battle of Cowpen. The night was pitch-dark and a violent storm was brewing in the Piedmont, just like in the preceding week. The creek beds and rivers were running hard, and water was running fast. Suddenly a loud thumping on the door jolted Jesse to alarm. As Jesse eased the door open in hesitation, wind, water and an escaped prisoner flooded into the entry. Rain hit the floor as the man half-gasped, half-shouted a warning that the British were moving to attack Baron Von Steuben and his 800 men. The men weren't just at stake; the site was home to a wealthy arsenal at Point of Fork, just above the confluence of the James and Rivanna Rivers. With the storm continuing on outside, Jesse knew he had to be quick if he was to avert the British attack. He yelled for his slave, Cuff, to mount Fearnaught (or Dreadnaught, as the official plaque reads), Thomas's famed thoroughbred. In haste, Cuff had Fearnaught ready. Jesse bounded out the door and onto the horse in what seemed a singular motion. Grasping the reigns with all the force he could muster despite his war injury, the duo dashed into the saturated darkness. The first impending danger was the turbulent Willis River, but the bridge remained intact despite the torrents beneath. With nostrils flaring, the horse bounded across the Willis River Bridge in a mere three strides. Racing through the dark forestland and forging through the sheets of rain, the two soon came to the "big river" named after King James I of England. With no ferry or bridge nearby, Thomas urged Fearnaught into the raging currents. The pair survived the crossing, and warned Von Steuben of Cornwallis's approach. A tale truly worthy of a roadside plaque!

World-famous Charles Dickens Visits Cumberland County

Charles Dickens was another famous visitor to the park, and many come to visit the nearby state forest to view the tombstone of Charles Irving Thornton, an infant boy who was born to Anthony and M.I. Thornton and died a mere 13 months and 19 days later. Recorded in the National Register of Historic Places and the Virginia Landmarks Register, this young lad's epitaph was written by Charles Dickens. How did this come about for a Virginia family living in such a remote area of the Commonwealth? Apparently, Mr. Dickens had been a recent visitor to the area, and this caught the attention of Thornton's attending physician, Dr. Deane, who promptly penned a personal request for a tombstone inscription. The good doctor's request was denied, and it was not until Mrs. Thornton wrote Dickens a second request that he agreed. No one knows for sure how many such requests the famed author received in his life, but this epitaph is only one of two ever written by Dickens, and the only one in the United States. The epitaph reads:

THIS IS THE GRAVE of a Little Child whom God in his goodness called to a Bright Eternity when he was very young. Hard as it is for Human Affection to reconcile itself to

Death in any shape [and most of all, perhaps at First In this] HIS PARENTS can even now believe (sic) that it will be a Consolation to them throughout their lives and when they shall have grown old and grey always to think of him as a child IN HEAVEN

"And Jesus called a little Child unto him, and set him in the midst of them."

He was the son of ANTHONY and M.I. THORNTON

Called CHARLES IRVING.

He was born on the 20th day of January 1841, and he died on the 12th day of March 1842. Having lived only 13 months and 19 days.

GHOSTLY AXE AT THE CABIN COMPLEX

Nearly all overnight visitors express gratitude after a quiet night at Bear Creek Lake State Park, however, some remark about odd sounds heard near Cabin 2 in the middle of the night. Whether they enjoy their stay in this particular cabin (or one next to it), visitors usually have an opinion about their stay. To anyone's knowledge, nothing terrible or sinister has occurred at the cabin or the land beneath the cabin, yet visitors repeatedly mention eerie and unexplained sounds occurring in the middle of the night, and accounts of these happenings have even been recorded in the cabin journals.

Guests usually emphasize the park's beautiful surroundings, but if you read between the lines of the journal entries, you sense so much more, particularly with Cabin 2 and the tales of a ghostly axe.

As nightfall reaches that magical hour of midnight, a permeable deadness descends in the Piedmont of Virginia. Stillness grasps the moist night air as minutes tick by, inching ever closer to 3 a.m., when the veil between the spirit and the human world is reputed to be thinnest. Suddenly an audible and unexplained thumping of an axe breaks the silence. Rhythmically, the mysterious sound is heard in Cabin 2. *Chop, chop, chop.* Thump after thump after thump, and then *crack* goes the wood as it splits in half and hits the ground with a sharp thud. Then again, *chop, chop, chop* all over again then *crack*, another split log hits the ground with a resounding thud. As the realization of what is occurring outside the cabin window resonates with the visitor, they hunker down in the bed sheets envisioning the slow rise of an axe by a ghostly hand. Repeatedly and undeniably, the chopping noise is heard. Shaking off the thought of a ghost, the visitor will rise and look out the window only to not see a soul. When daybreak unfolds, the visitor will search for any signs of freshly chopped wood, wood chips, or even the impression of footsteps, only to walk away with no explanation of the mysterious sound.

Some may disregard this clamor as an echo coming from another cabin dweller gathering and splitting wood in an attempt to defray the night's chill. However, all the cabins have gas fireplaces and the task of chopping wood is unnecessary. The disbeliever may discount this noise thinking its origin comes from across the lake at the campground, but why would a camper split wood in the middle of the night, and when pre-split firewood is readily available to campers?

Just a short distance away rests the quiet overgrown cemetery where young Charles Irving Thornton rests. Perhaps the sounds come from his father, who is keen on keeping the night fires ablaze as his son gradually drifts to death's dark doorstep. Or perhaps it's Cuff, Jesse Thomas's slave, relentlessly at work to keep his master and his horse, Fearnaught, prepared for another bout of harsh weather and fearless act of gallantry. One thing is for sure, the spirit is a presence that insists on keeping the home fires burning.

CABIN JOURNALS

If illusionary wood chopping does not unravel the nerves of Bear Creek Lake guests, then the spirit finds other ways to manifest its existence. Captured in the cabin journals are several well-documented and unsettling encounters. The first notable oddity occurred in Spring 2007 when a Northern Virginia family exclaimed, "We met a ghost in this cabin; it kept turning on the faucets at night and kept sitting in Jim's bed. Pretty scary."

Humorous paranormal encounters occur too. One such account comes from a group of adults, who described the resident ghosts as "hunters of children." "On the last day we figured out that Cabin 2 was haunted and saw a ghost. The ghost was four feet tall. At night he goes from bedroom to bedroom groaning and looking for little children to eat." Soon afterward the cabin is host to folks who obviously lack belief in the supernatural. "Thank you previous guests for the warnings about the night sounds. We slept much sounder knowing what they were, ceiling fans as well as the fridge."

It was February 2008 when the ghost decided a few mischievous tricks were in store for the next arrivals. They briefly chronicle, "Beware of the ghost. It opens peanut jars when they are closed and turns on the faucet. Oooohhh!" Curiously, within a month, a male guest takes the ghostly phenomena seriously. "So there has been mention of this place being haunted. Our second night we turned in early 10:30 p.m. or so. Around 12:30 a.m. I strolled to the bathroom. We had the night light on in the bathroom for guidance since there was no moonlight to guide our way. I sat down on the toilet so as to be quiet and not wake my wife. Suddenly I heard three slow thumps. My ears perked up trying to locate the origin of the sound. The thumps sounded deep. The many explanations of this sound started racing through my mind: someone chopping wood far off, someone locked out of a nearby cabin, but just as the option popped into my head that I had imagined the thumps, I heard them again. I convinced myself that they were caused by a neighbor and went back to sleep. This morning my wife was reading this journal out loud and mentioned the ghost. I then remembered what happened last night and now using an awake brain, I can only tell you that the thumps sounded like someone hitting the side of their fist against a stone wall."

As time passes and the journals compile a harrowing list of frightful and distressing tales, it is March 2008 when a Northern Virginia family arrived for a similar experience, but with a twist. They inscribe details of the eerie manifestations of an otherworldly subject that quietly lurked about the cabin, creating odd scratching sounds as it moved about before entering one of the bedrooms and sitting at the foot of the bed. No one was seen but the distinct feeling of a body's weight could be felt at the end of the bed for a brief time.

As Spring 2008 unfolded, a couple from Richmond, Virginia, continue with the tales, "No ghost sightings but when we woke up Sunday there was a very thin walking stick on the back porch near the stairway; it wasn't ours so beware."

One thing is for sure: the seemingly shadowy soul that slips around the area of Cabin 2 seems fascinated with wood. With this in mind, could the quest for more firewood come from old Mr. Thornton's spirit that remains grieving the loss of his infant son? Or could it be the ghost of Jesse Thomas or even Cuff, whose unsettled nerves shiver from that fateful night? Perchance the restlessness arises from a spirit belonging to a long-ago farmer simply tending to a daily task, but whatever the cause, it's been heard by many.

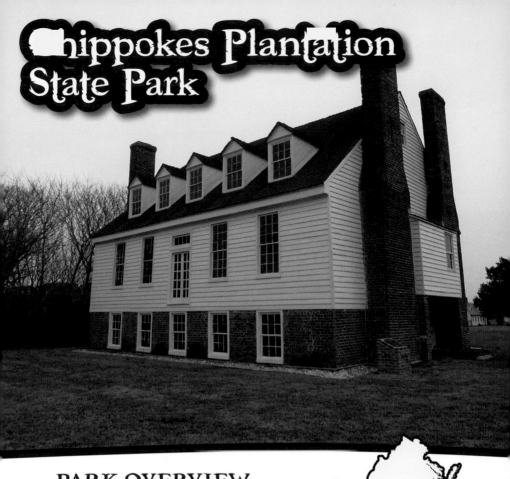

Chippokes Plantation State Park

PARK OVERVIEW

ACRES: 1,947   **FOUNDED:** 1967

NEARBY: Colonial Williamsburg, Jamestown Settlement, York-town Victory Center, Historic James River, Bacon's Castle, Albert C. Jones cemetery, York River State Park

NOTABLE VISITORS: Thomas Jefferson, Captain William Powell, Lucy Ludwell Paradise, Albert C. Jones Family, Governor Mills E. Godwin

ABOUT THE PARK

The historic Chippokes Plantation is located on the quiet side of Virginia's "Historic Triangle," which consists of Colonial Williamsburg, the Jamestown Settlement and

Yorktown Victory Center. Off the beaten path, the area is home to some of the Commonwealth's most historic sites, including several Colonial-era living-history museums.

Chippokes Plantation is a short ferry ride from Jamestown. A pastoral and scenic setting, the state park is affectionately referred to by former Park Manager William Jacobs as a "jewel on the James, an inexpensive place to camp but a treasure to behold." Resting opposite Jamestown Island, the plantation has yielded crops for more than four hundred years; over its lifetime, the site has witnessed everything from the early days of the Colony to the rise of the Commonwealth and slavery to the Civil War and Reconstruction.

Today, the park is a center for recreational activities; features include a campground, historic yet modernly equipped cabins, an Olympic-sized swimming pool, numerous historic buildings including the antebellum Jones-Stewart mansion, well-tended gardens, and miles of scenic trails created for hikers, bikers and horseback riders. The site is also home to the Chippokes Farm & Forestry Museum, which provides a look at the technology of the past. Year-round interpretive programming brings the area's history and culture to life. The park's wildlife is lovely as well. The nineteen hundred-acre site is home to a myriad of mammals, birds and other animals.

PARK HISTORY

A Long History

The name Chippokes stems from the name of Choupoke, an Algonquin Chief, who was friendly to the early colonists and credited with helping the settlers survive. The first English owner of the property was Captain William Powell, captain of the Jamestown Fort. Powell was granted 550 acres of river frontage on Chippokes Creek in 1619. Captain

Powell bequeathed the property to his son in 1645, who in turn sold it to Henry Bishop in 1646. Mr. Bishop purchased some adjacent property, bringing the plantation to a total of 1,900 acres. From 1684 through 1827 the family of Philip Ludwell III owned the property. They did not reside on-site but nearby in the colonial capital of Williamsburg, a much more suitable location for a prominent member of London society and one who held a position on the Governor's Council. His daughter, Lucy Ludwell, is believed to haunt the Ludwell-Paradise House, which is a popular attraction within Colonial Williamsburg.

Upon her father's passing, Lucy became the beneficiary of the property. Two years later Lucy married John Paradise, the son of prominent Peter Paradise, former British consul at Salonica in Macedonia. The young couple were of London's highest social class and their future was destined for wealth and fame.

Lucy was even a friend of Thomas Jefferson. While Ambassador to the Court of Versailles in 1788, Jefferson wrote, "We are personally and well acquainted with the family of Mrs. Lucy Paradise, wife of John Paradise . . . her ancestors . . . have been most distinguished."

However, Lucy was notoriously loose with her finances. She ultimately became destitute soon after John's death in 1795. With nowhere else to go, Lucy Ludwell Paradise returned to the Ludwell-Paradise Home in Williamsburg. Perhaps it was her very unhappy marriage to an overly mild-mannered man, or her disappointment with her financial status, or just the fact that Lucy was often thought to be quite a nasty person, but soon she became known as an eccentric and was called "Loony Lucy." Harboring delusional thoughts of royalty, Lucy Ludwell frequently strolled down the town's brick pathways along Duke of Gloucester Street, followed by servants, and giving a "royal" wave to the passersby. Her eccentricity soon worsened and she developed a propensity for walking directly into neighbors' homes and stealing clothing. Not mortified in the least, she would wear the stolen garb and stroll throughout the village. Residents were patient at first but Lucy's dominating personality wore on their nerves, especially when she insisted others join her in illusionary carriage rides, where her servants rocked the carriage and she gave the royal wave, believing she was back in London. By 1816, the townspeople reached their limit and five men hauled poor, confused Lucy to the nearest asylum. Kicking and screaming the entire way, she declared someday she would return home. Indeed many believe Lucy did just that. When the property underwent major renovation work, the workers reported missing tools, scattered papers, water turning on and off by itself and loud banging noises throughout the residence. They even claim to have heard noises of splashing water as if someone was taking a bath. Lucy apparently was more than a kooky kleptomaniac; she was also a clean freak.

Through the centuries, Chippokes Plantation continued to change hands but never served as a primary residence. Albert C. Jones became the owner in 1837. His family plot, now encircled by crumbling brick walls, lies several miles south of the park along Rt. 10. As the first owner to reside on the plantation, the River House was his home until 1854, when he built a larger brick home in the Classical Italianate style, and it is now known as the Jones-Stewart Mansion. However, Mr. Jones is said to have preferred to live in the River House, which provided a bird's-eye view over several slave quarters, one of which now houses the park manager.

Eventually the property matured into a homestead of 20 buildings, including two plantation houses, slave quarters, and a number of farm buildings. The plantation remained in the Jones family until 1916, at which point it was in a state of disrepair and went to public auction. Fortunately, Mr. and Mrs. Victor Stewart purchased the site, and over four decades lovingly restored all the amenities, thus recapturing the essence of the original plantation. Following Victor's death, Mrs. Stewart donated the property to the Commonwealth of Virginia for a state park that would be a lasting memorial to Victor. One of her requirements was that the mansion's furnishings must remain as they were during their lives.

A HAUNTED HISTORY

As the park system developed and expanded its interpretive programs, Chippokes became one of many destinations in Virginia where visitors could hear tales of colonial life. The tales are varied and often involve the paranormal. This is especially true at Chippokes Plantation State Park, where mysterious sightings and encounters are often reported. A number of rental cabins are reputedly hot spots of paranormal activity, and visitors often report colorful encounters with spirits. These ghostly encounters have been passed down at the park, becoming an oral history of spooky tales.

THE JONES-STEWART MANSION

While visitors are invited during normal park hours to meander at their leisure through the historic gardens outside the Jones-Stewart Mansion, the mansion is also open for tours. One tour happened to coincide with an outbreak of nasty weather, and no one showed up. The tour that day was to be led by a fairly new docent by the name of Joan Miller, who was accompanied by her husband Bill. All alone, the pair were growing hungry when Bill decided to run to town for carry-out. Mrs. Miller recalls the experience: "A long time ago, Bill and I were here at the mansion and the exterior of the mansion was under renovation. They were removing paint, and reviewing and studying the architecture. Scaffolds and all sorts of equipment were about. They were saying that the front of the house had always been white but were thinking of changing the color because they found dark red colors underneath. Someone said Mrs. Stewart always liked white and would turn over in her grave if they painted it another color. It was a dark and dank day; Bill decided he would go to the shopping center for pizza. I was in the front hall of the mansion sitting in a chair by myself. Suddenly the double doors burst open and wind came rushing in and whatever 'it' was: a mix of hair and transparent mist whirled into the entryway and careened down the hallway and out the other side." Mrs. Miller reported knowing she should get up to close the doors and stop the cold wind but she was physically unable to do so. Mrs. Miller didn't recall seeing a face but was amazed at the unexplained sight. The apparition was "human-sized, very visual, a dazzling display of ethereal loveliness."

Most stories about paranormal phenomena at the mansion are kept hush-hush, but some stories slip out. One such manifestation is the repeated tale of shadowy apparitions, presumably the Stewarts, rocking methodically in the chairs on the side porch. Time and again, park guests ask about the smiling individuals dressed in period clothing rocking on the side porch. At first the docents were puzzled, but they are now accustomed to the inquiries and no longer peek out onto the porch because they know not a soul will be in sight.

A PLEASANT AROMA IN THE STUDY

Touring guests also inquire about the frequent aroma of tobacco smoke in the first floor study. Again puzzled, volunteers occasionally check more closely, even picking up Mr. Stewart's pipe, which inevitably is odorless and cold. Mrs. Stewart is also apparently fastidious about the placement of their many books. No matter where a borrowed book is left, they always peculiarly return to their original niche, without ever having been moved by volunteers.

HISTORIC BRICK KITCHEN

A volunteer corps, the Friends of Chippokes Plantation formed in 1988; it is a small but passionate group of citizens who have dedicated thousands of hours of time and effort to enhancing park visitor experiences. With so much time spent in the park, they have also experienced the most extraordinary and unexplainable happenings.

This is true for a young volunteer by the name of Derek. Long familiar with the eerie rumors about the park, he didn't think too much about the stories until he found himself in the midst of one. It all began a short distance across the mansion yard in the two-story detached brick kitchen, which is the site of the park's hearth-cooking demonstrations.

On a particularly calm day, Derek Jr. found himself alone in the brick kitchen when he heard flute music upstairs. Thinking someone left a radio on, he went upstairs but couldn't find a radio or anything else that could have made the sound. Thinking it strange, he listened more and was sure it was a flute. He suddenly realized he was experiencing ghostly activity. Lurching for the staircase, he grabbed the railing and hoisted himself downward to the first floor and out the nearest door. With his heart pounding, he blazed across the yard toward a small group of volunteers. Derek gasped for breath. With a broken voice he sputtered, "Did you hear that, did you hear that, did you hear someone playing a flute?" There was no doubt in anyone's mind that Derek had experienced something out of the ordinary.

Derek's mother, Dee Van den Brink, was a seasoned volunteer at Chippokes and all too familiar with the ghostly encounters. In fact, Mrs. Van den Brink speaks of a time when she and her husband were working the Christmas Show, just one of numerous events held at Chippokes. Mrs. Van den Brink was alone reading the newspaper in the brick kitchen when she heard footsteps outside. It was unusual to have a passerby stroll past the kitchen without stopping in. With that in mind, she rose to peek outside. She did so only to discover no one was there. No staff, no volunteer, and no park guest were remotely close to the kitchen.

THE SMITH HOUSE

Another location that is frequented by shadowy spirits is the Old Smith House. Over a hundred and fifty years ago, the white clapboard structure served as slave quarters. It is within the walls of this structure that former Park Manager Danette Poole and her relatives experienced chilling paranormal activity, and her children saw apparitions on more than one occasion.

One of Poole's first experiences occurred not long after she gave birth to her son, Jerry. A short time after Jerry's birth, she fell ill. With a newborn in her arms and fighting off an illness, her sister-in-law took sympathy and made the journey to serve as a caregiver. It was a sacrifice, because she too was a young mother and left her son behind with his father. After a few days, the sister-in-law's husband called and said their one-and-a-half-year-old son was in need of his mother. Shortly thereafter, the young lad came to visit, but he seemed unusually agitated from the onset. Mrs. Poole and her sister-in-law both thought it odd because the boy was typically a calm and pleasant child. After the mother's endless attempts to settle the child down, Mrs. Poole reassured her sister-in-law that Jerry was fast asleep and that she was feeling a bit better, and she encouraged her to attend to her own son. Both mother and child went upstairs and lay on a bed and soon both were comfortably asleep. It was a brief rest as the sister-in-law found herself aroused by a strange feeling. She looked over at her son, and found him staring up toward the ceiling smiling and quietly jabbering, as young children often do. She casually rolled over and looked in the same direction. Numb in disbelief, she could not believe her eyes. There stood a lean black man dressed in all white. He held his finger to his mouth as if to say "hush" and began to speak directly to her son. Even though the voice was inaudible, she presumed his words were words of comfort since her son was not anxious. Remaining deathly quiet, she kept staring at him, and moments later the man vaporized before their eyes. Freaked out by the experience, she hastily grabbed her son and flew down the staircase to tell of her unnerving experience. Remarkably, for the remainder of their stay, the child was at peace.

A MYSTERIOUS DUO

Now serving as the residence for the park manager and her family, the old slave quarters structure left room for imagination when it came to housing a family of four. With the creative talents of Mrs. Poole's husband, the utility room became a nursery. One night, mom tucked Jerry snug into his loft bed, then settled into her bed below. Feeling something was amiss, she woke up to find Jerry staring down, toward the room's window. When she asked her son if he was all right, he replied that he was fine, just watching the women seated in the chair brushing one another's hair. Mrs. Poole said "OK, that's fine" and lay back down to sleep. The next morning over breakfast she asked for more details about the ladies. In child-like fashion the young boy described the ladies who were dressed in colonial attire and merrily combing each other's long tresses. One has to wonder what Jerry really saw. Was it two spirits or just Jerry's clothing tossed on the chair casting shadows in the moonlight?

THINGS THAT GO BUMP
IN THE NIGHT

Virginia's state parks have had overnight cabins available for guests since the 1930s. They are popular with many folks who want to experience the park after dark and through the night. When the state was developing plans for campgrounds and cabins at Chippokes, the historic structures associated with the plantation seemed perfect for repurposing.

Three of the parks wonderfully appointed cabins were once home to generations of Osborne, Brown and Spratley family members. These families were originally brought to the area as slaves; successive generations worked as tenant farmers and even as staff members at the park. The families all originated from Angola, and were brought to Jamestown, where they were essential.

Given this awful history, it's no wonder that stories abound about paranormal sightings and peculiar activity at the park. Sometime in the 1990s the state park system began installing journals in each cabin, encouraging people to chronicle their experiences. Over the years a few unsettling journal entries have graced the pages of these journals.

One account reads:

> My name is Philip Jones of New York, 51 years old. I brought three generations of my family and extended family members to Chippokes Plantation to find our origin. I have been researching my family genealogy for about seven years and have confirmed my origin on this trip: my family came from Angola on the continent of Africa, almost four hundred years ago.
>
> How? Well a ship called the *Treasurer* of the Virginia Company of London sailed from Jamestown, Virginia, in the summer of 1618 to gather food and supplies. Somewhere offshore, the *Treasurer* joined

forces with a Dutch vessel and captured a Spanish frigate destined for the Spanish West Indies. A search of the captured frigate found no gold, silver or food, but it was loaded with several hundred Africans, who were dumped in the *Treasurer's* hatches.

Adverse winds overtook the *Treasurer* and the Dutch ship on their way back to Jamestown, Virginia. The storm caused them to lose one another, and a shortage of food on the ship led them to dump many Africans overboard. Only about 22 Africans arrived in Jamestown. The *Treasurer* returned alone and the colony of Jamestown claimed the cargo of the first Africans to arrive here in America, and they were my Angolan ancestors.

Since then my family were slaves, servants, indentured servants, and eventually free citizens and government employees of Chippokes Plantation. The state of Virginia recognized their contributions by naming their homes, now cabins, after my family: The Osborne House, Brown House and Spratley House.

Today my son and granddaughter are staying in the cabin that was my cousin's (the Spratley House), and me and my daughter, two granddaughters and one grandson are staying in another cousin's house (the Brown House). These are the same homes where my family gave birth, slept, ate, worked and had fun.

Yes, there are spirits in these cabins; my Grandmother Louise Osborne told me stories of strange things happening in Chippokes that cannot be explained, strange sounds and sights. We heard these sounds and have seen unexplainable sights of people, working, walking and talking. Once when we returned from a trip to Virginia Beach, at night, we saw people sitting at the table eating. We saw them and wondered what they were doing in our cabin. But when we got closer, they disappeared.

Another incident occurred when my granddaughter was acting up and was sent upstairs. Once there, the lamp fell off the table, and she tried to scream but couldn't. Instead a voice and image came out of the wall and said, "Behave yourself." She ran downstairs and told us the story, and she was very well behaved for the rest of our stay, but she never went back upstairs.

There are many stories of slaves returned to haunt their captors, but what happened to us was different. Our family was letting us know that they are here, that we are still family in life or in spirit."

THE SPRATLEY HOUSE

Embracing the fall splendor in October 2006, Cabin 1 (also referred to as the Spratley House) welcomed new guests who happened to be looking forward to a pleasantly cool afternoon hike and an opportunity to catch up. The moment was short-lived. Foul weather descended on the park and the couple found themselves huddled in the house longer than desired. The pair writes "rumor has it the Spratley House is haunted. This being close to Halloween, I must warn you, the bed in the spare bedroom shakes at night; there are strange noises and doors will open and shut by themselves. Once, the front door locked on its own. Also, the thermostat seems to change by itself and the electricity will flicker from time to time."

Interestingly, with All Hallows' Eve only hours away, the last entry for October is direct, "Beware! This cabin is haunted! One of the beds shakes when you are sleeping. It happened to me. Pennies will start to fall from the ceiling!

The rocking chair will start to rock and the lights will flicker! Sometimes the door will lock on its own. So . . . *beware!*"

Many other entries cataloged similar occurrences. Taken together, they emphatically conclude "Believe It! This place is haunted!"

Another account tells of a family gathered around reading the ghostly tales and deciding to put the ghost to the test. Before leaving for the day's recreation, they placed a circle of pennies on the kitchen table and upon returning they couldn't believe what they saw: the pennies were now in the shape of a square.

By year's end, the journal was chock-full of entries confirming paranormal activity. Encounters range from peculiar noises and restless pets to sequential raps above and below the beds to mysteriously rearranged objects and glimpses of disembodied spirits. Amazingly, visitors keep coming back to the cabin and enjoy their time there, despite the haunting presences.

THE BROWN HOUSE

Cabin 2, the Brown House (built circa 1850), served as an overseer's residence and now finds itself the center of supernatural activity. Reports of rocking chairs moving to different locations within a room are not uncommon. On a number of occasions, guests have been known to arrive at Cabin 2 and think they either have the wrong cabin or the wrong vacation date because a family appears to be enjoying a meal at the kitchen table. Inevitably, the newly arrived guests knock at the door but no one answers, so they enter the cabin only to find it empty. Cabin 2 is also infamous for the repeated appearance who is said to gaze out the second-story window.

Chippokes' gregarious housekeeper, Mrs. Shirley Roberg, recalls a time when her daughter Abigail was helping her clean this particular cabin. Abigail was upstairs working and laid her iPod on the bed and walked several feet away. Its screen went off and went into lock mode. As Abigail continued tidying up the room, suddenly her iPod lit up. As she watched in disbelief, her private passcode was punched in. Abigail screamed as she raced down the steps.

Other stories seem to coincide with nightfall. Strange creaking noises and thumps are often reported emanating from upstairs. Guests reluctantly climb the slender stairs in search of the source of the muffled sounds. Peeking into the small upstairs bedroom, most believe the odd sounds come from an area near the fireplace. As you can see from this photograph, there appears to be an orb or even an ethereal figure in the exact location reported by the guests.

And so, it seems no matter where you are at the park, it's likely you will glimpse the unusual. But despite these apparent apparitions, Chippokes Plantation remains a peaceful respite for those living in the present day, and maybe for those from days passed, too.

Douthat State Park

PARK OVERVIEW

ACRES: 4,493   **FOUNDED:** 1936

NEARBY: The Homestead, Clifton Forge Railroad Museum, Alleghany Arts and Crafts Center, Falling Springs Falls, Historic Lexington, Natural Bridge Park

NOTABLE VISITORS: U.S. Senators Teddy Kennedy and Tim Kaine

ABOUT THE PARK

Lying between two massive mountain ridges, Douthat State Park is listed on the Virginia Landmark Register and the National Register of Historic Places. It is well known for its historic cabins and restaurant overlooking a 50-acre trout-stocked lake. Three lodges accommodate larger groups while three campgrounds accommodate tenters, RV users and equestrians. Forty-three miles of trail, ranging from easy to difficult, weave through rhododendron and mountain laurel glens, leading to hundreds of miles of trail in the George Washington and Jefferson National Forest.

An Old Friend

Douthat State Park was the first Virginia state park my family ever visited. The year was 1986 and our boys were two and five years old. We camped in a small tent in a beautiful lakeside site with a panoramic view of Douthat Lake. That first visit was a fun and inspirational one and we were camped next to an older couple from Christiansburg. They took an interest in our boys and shared with us some homemade jam and local honey. We remember thinking that Virginians were very hospitable; we imagined it was the world-famous southern hospitality at work. It wasn't exactly what we had encountered growing up in northeast Ohio, where the pace of life seemed much faster and people were less considerate.

PARK HISTORY

The history of the park is fascinating. Its opens a window to the lifestyle of these mountain folk and their love of the rolling blue misty mountains and laurel-studded crevices that lead down to the populated valleys. Clean spring waters cascade from the Allegheny Highlands and the waters teem with rainbow trout: a fly fisherman's lifeblood.

A Chronicled Past

This beautiful, expansive park is nestled in the Allegheny Highlands of the southern Appalachian range. Douthat was the first state park acquired when the Commonwealth was just getting into the state park business. It was named for

Robert Douthat, a landowner from the 1700s. The Douthat Land Company donated over 1,900 acres along the gorge of the Nelson River in Bath and Alleghany Counties; the state soon bought another 2,500 acres for $50,000—a remarkable investment.

Home to three Civilian Conservation Corps camps in the 1930s, the park has retained much of the design of the original camps and their structures, and it has consequently been designated a National Historic District. There were three CCC camps at Douthat: Camp Douthat, Camp Malone and Camp Carson. Most of the CCC members hailed from Pennsylvania. Camp Douthat built the cabins and roads, Camp Malone managed the forest and trail construction and Camp Carson built the rock spillway, the dam and the lake itself.

Douthat was also one of the first parks to offer electricity to its customers. The first cabins had a coin-activated system: put in a dime, turn the knob and the power was on, and the lights showcased the beautiful timber-and-stone craftsmanship. This would have been a pretty amazing experience for many people in the 1930s. Some areas of the Commonwealth didn't get electric power until after World War II. Originally the power came from a local hydroelectric project, one of the first in the region.

STAINED HISTORY

Unfortunately, life in the mountains isn't always exciting. Especially for those stuck in a remote cabin, boredom could be a problem. This was one of the primary reasons the area was dotted with taverns. In fact, the original Douthat Lakeview Restaurant was called The Tavern and old-timers in the area still refer to it as such. (It is well documented that boredom and substance abuse go hand in hand.) Folks sure loved their parks, but many found other pastimes, and drinking was one of them. And it was not just the average citizen who tipped the bottle too frequently. On one such occasion, it was a trusted, civil servant—the park's manager.

The entrance road to Douthat is lined with trees, including some truly ancient specimens. It was one of those enormous old trees that sent the spirit of a 1950s park manager straight to heaven.

At the time, Douthat Lake entertained several fishermen, a handful of cabin guests, and a smattering of hikers. He headed out to a local gathering place to catch up on the news—a form of "social media" back in the day. Calling back to the park office, he learned all was well at Douthat State Park, so he figured no harm would come if he indulged. Indulge he did, to the point of becoming too drunk to drive.

Feeling no pain, the park manager stumbled into his Ford Ranchero and headed up Douthat Road. The Ford swerved around the first curve, then the second, then the third. Eventually, the curves seemed endless and turning the wheel this way and that way became more difficult, especially without power steering. He tugged the wheel right, leaning into the forested curve. Then he tugged it back left. Neighbors recall hearing the tires squeal.

He slammed straight into an old oak tree. The manager's body broke against the steering wheel and his head struck the windshield, shattering it. The perilous curve snatched his life.

"Stone cold dead" is how the state police described the park manager. His family and friends wept at the service when he was buried, but some locals claim that he wasn't exactly at rest. Tales abound about an oddly attired geezer in green-and-tan garb at the intersection of the forest road and Douthat Road, the site where the manager gasped his last breath.

UNEXPLAINED TRESPASSERS

Car accidents aren't exactly uncommon in the area given the twisting and turning mountain roads. But it's rare for a pair of car accidents to occur at exactly the same place. But two teenagers died exactly where the park manager died. They were zooming at a high rate of speed out of the park and headed down to Clifton Forge, a bustling railroad town.

Unlike the park manager's ghost, these two teens don't stand stoically. Instead, they frolic about the woods and talk and laugh and carry on as if a grand future waits. Are these the boisterous, youthful voices of the dead? No one is sure, not even the park staff, who occasionally get called to investigate the ruckus caused by what is believed to be trespassing teens. The park police calls always end the same: no trespassers are ever found, and there's no evidence anyone just fled the scene.

RELIABLE SOURCE EXPERIENCES THE UNEXPLAINED

Back in the day, when the current manager, Charlie Conner, was a seasonal worker, he pulled the graveyard shift. It was the wee hours of the morning when he experienced something he'll never forget. He headed up the side of the mountain to check on Douthat Lodge. Nestled in a forest of hemlock and rhododendron, the quaint structure appears to be much smaller in size than it actually is; the building contains six spacious bedrooms.

Knowing the lodge was unoccupied, he made a pass to ensure no one was lurking about. He arrived to find a light shining from the front right window. Getting out of the parked vehicle, nothing felt uncomfortable or unusual until he placed his key in the door and heard the door unlock, by itself. Focusing his thoughts to keep fear from taking over, he gently pushed on the front door.

The ranger entered the room where the light was on, and he promptly turned it off. With haste he bounced outside and shone his flashlight to each side of the building but found nothing and no one. He returned to his vehicle and headed back down the mountain.

As the night wore on he circled back again to check the campground, cabins and then climb the mountainside for another check of the lodge. He was stunned in disbelief, the light was back on! Ranger Conner was sure someone was lurking inside and upon hearing his arrival, he figured they scurried away to a back bedroom. Focusing at the task before him, he bounded out of the vehicle but unexpectedly was immediately struck with a haunting feeling that raised goose bumps on his arms. But when he entered the lodge and surveyed the premises, he found nothing amiss. Now wondering if the light was an electrical problem he thought it best to unplug the light.

After locking up, he left, and a few hours later, his patrol brought him to the Douthat Lodge again. He couldn't believe what he saw: the same light in the same room was on.

This time Ranger Conner didn't re-enter the lodge. A later investigation by the park's maintenance team never found an electrical problem.

SECRETS UNFOLD

Years ago, my husband was hiking at the park when he wandered into a primitive cabin along Tuscarora Overlook

Trail. There he found a decrepit old man in dirty, tattered clothing and with long, scraggly steely hair that framed his skeletal, weather-worn face. He sat on the floor, leaning against the back wall. Babbling to himself, he made no indication of noticing my husband. My husband claims the gibbering sounded as if it was directed to someone or something in the shelter that only he could see or hear. Joe quickly left and hurried down the trail to join up with our group. Ever since, he refers to the strange man in the cabin as "Grizzly Man."

The cabin where Grizzly Man was spotted is well known among the park staff who note that it's often lit up at night. This in itself wouldn't be so unusual, but the cabin has no access to electricity. What's more, the trail that leads to it is rock-strewn and difficult, hardly the place for a midnight hike.

Another interesting tidbit about the place is when curious staffers and volunteers venture up the mountainside to inspect the cabin, they never can keep a candle lit within the walls of this cabin. The candle immediately goes out. Even when the door is closed and not a breeze is felt, the candle will promptly go out, as if someone has blown it out.

ANOTHER HAUNTED LOCALE

The Tavern, as some old-timers still call it, was built just after the Great Depression and has entertained mountain travelers for nearly 80 years. Today it's a popular place to enjoy good food and a good atmosphere. But that wasn't always the case. Unfortunately long ago someone made the mistake of hiring a cantankerous old woman to manage the camp store that adjoins the restaurant.

Skinny as a skeleton and rather slovenly in appearance, she somehow landed the job as the storekeeper. Disruptive and unpleasant to all who passed through the doors, she also ventured over into the restaurant from time to time. Most staff ignored the old crank. Uninvited, she would rearrange the kitchen equipment, making a racket in the process. Inevitably the staff would call security, who'd remove her. This process repeated until she eventually died on-site many years later—no one knows exactly why. So when visitors report the unexplained sound of cutlery clattering and pots rattling, park staff joke—with a hint of truth—that the sound is caused by the soul of the crotchety old woman.

A FORMER EMPLOYEE SHARES THE LEGEND OF JONATHAN ROSE

It was 2013 when Tom Cervenack retired after 25 years with the Virginia State Parks system. He shares a harrowing tale of his days as Douthat Park Manager and why he applied for a transfer out of the park. In the words of Tom:

"My first park was here at Douthat State Park in the fall of 1986, but by the summer 1987, I wanted out! It has to do with something that happened here shortly after my arrival. At the time there was an occupied parcel of land (now within the park boundaries at Douthat) that covered about 50 acres of land and had a two-story wooden house with a brick fireplace and a big porch. It was the home of Martha and Abraham Rose and their 10-year-old son Jonathan. Jonathan wasn't like the other kids, and that was probably the reason he was asked to leave school and was home-schooled. Many described Jonathan as a wild boy with a love for the land and its creatures but little tolerance for humans. He was gifted in many ways, but also incredibly odd. He had an incredible sense of smell, could run and leap like a deer and hunt like a wolf. But Jonathan reportedly had a birth defect: webbed toes. He spent most of his time running through the woods, sleeping outdoors for a night or two at a time. Martha and Abraham had trouble controlling him and his temper, and that is likely the reason they avoided telling him a little secret. You see, Abraham had lost his job at the mill in Covington and was finding it harder and harder to make ends meet. When the state came to them with a very generous offer for the property and house, he sold it and used the money to buy a new house in Roanoke, where he had also secured a new job at a factory. But he knew the news would be crushing to Jonathan, so Martha and Abraham waited until two days before they were to move to break the news to Jonathan.

The results were even worse than they expected. Jonathan went into a terrible rage when he heard that his property was going to become part of the state park. He swore *revenge on each and every person to set foot on the land.*

Several people in the community came to help them pack. At one point during the evening, the group moved to the barn to begin packing things there. About 8 p.m. they heard blood-curdling screams coming from the house. To their horror, the house was in flames and Jonathan was trapped inside. The blistering flames prevented them from entering. With only a well on the property and the fire department a half an hour away, they could do nothing but watch. Within minutes, Jonathan's cries ceased and they knew they had lost their son.

The following morning the Clifton Forge and Covington Fire Marshals were on the scene and soon discovered that a flammable liquid was poured at both the front door and back door of the house and four of the windows. The fire was intentional. News quickly spread through town, shocking all that heard it. But the even bigger news was about to hit: the fire department never found a body or any remains at all.

Some say that Jonathan never died in that fire, despite the boy's screams. Some say he is still here, seeking revenge on each and every person that comes to visit his property, at the park. Some even say that would explain the farm animals that were found half-eaten, covered with bite marks. Farmers reported that the carcasses were torn apart, almost as if by human hands.

Jonathan's presence in the park would also explain the missing campers of 1992 and the "accidental" death of a hiker in '97. Officially, the hiker died after tripping and hitting his head on the rocks, but his body looked as if it had fallen off a 50-foot cliff.

There are several reasons I asked to be transferred in the spring of 1987, but I can tell you this, while walking on Wilson Creek Trail, something doesn't seem right, almost like I am being watched. Never do I see anything out of the ordinary, other than an occasional set of footprints, and they have webbed toes.

Hungry Mother State Park

PARK OVERVIEW

ACRES: 2,900   **FOUNDED:** 1936

NEARBY: Lincoln Theatre, Historic General Francis Marion Hotel and Black Rooster Gallery, Historic Saltville, Wolf Creek Indian Village and Museum, Virginia Heritage Music Trail

NOTABLE VISITORS: Governors George C. Perry and E. Lee Trinkle, Robert Fechner, director of the Civilian Conservation Corps in 1936

ABOUT THE PARK

Hungry Mother State Park was founded in 1936 when the land became the first segment of what is now a 36-park system in the Commonwealth of Virginia. The park features 15 hiking and biking trails, campgrounds for tenters and RVs, a conference center, an extensive cabin community, an impressive restaurant facility overlooking a 108-acre swimming and fishing lake, and a historic six-family log lodge.

PARK HISTORY

Hungry Mother: Where Did That Name Come From?

The name "Hungry Mother State Park" has been inspiration for countless songs, poems and ballads. Lore has it that the name came from a creek of the same name, which comes from a legend that is attributed to the American Indians in the region. While there are several different versions of the story, all involve a starving child calling out "hungry mammy." In a popular version of the tale, a woman named Molly was found dead with a starving child who was wailing the words "hungry mammy." Still another tale refers to a westward settler that left his wife and child behind. The abandoned pair wandered through the forest for days in a feeble attempt to reach relatives. The mother succumbed to hunger, perishing on the woodland floor as the child sat sobbing the sad words "hungry mammy."

But as the Historical Society writes, "none of these versions is correct," for land papers indicate that Molly Marley lived on the knob bearing the same name before these other events occurred. However, one version is more believable. It comes from the late Mr. Edward Copenhaver, who shares the account told by his grandmother, the wife of the first Copenhaver to inhabit the area. As the legend goes, the Indians attacked a settlement either on the New River or somewhere nearby, killing a man and taking his wife and child as prisoners. As they made their way down the Middle Fork of Holston Trail they were pursued by white settlers, and the woman and male child escaped. The woman marked her trail by using the old hikers' trick of breaking sticks and dropping them along the path. The pursuers followed her trail and found a weakened boy hugging the collapsed body of his mother. When they found him, he was crying "Hungry mammy, hungry mammy." The men carried mother and child to a nearby cabin. They never forgot the chilling wails of the starving child, and to this day, the stream is known as "Hungry Mother Creek."

Legend and lore abound about this mythical mother and child. According to the book *Hungry Mother: History and Legends* by deceased author Mack H. Sturgill, Sturgill uncovered a publication from 1932 that told yet another story. Titled *History and Traditions of Smyth County* and written by Goodridge Wilson, it states: "Surveys of 1774 by Robert and John Crow show that the stream had its unusual name that early, so if the story be true concerning a lost child found after several days' search on its banks who greeting rescuers with the words "Hungry Mother," it occurred prior to 1774." Local historian and President of the Friends of Hungry Mother State Park, John Taminger, tells the author about a map currently held at the state park office with the date 1899. It is on this map that the name Hungry Mother Creek is clearly printed.

The Twentieth Century

It was 1926 when the Commonwealth created the State Commission on Conservation and Development. William E. Carson served as the first chairman, and he conceived the idea of a state park system and development of Shenandoah National Park. Carson had no funds, just an endorsement by the members of the Commission, but he had a plan. He hired a landscape architect by the name of R.E. Burson for assistance in convincing the politicians and working-man alike. With the Depression looming over everything, Carson's task seemed insurmountable. Undeterred, he traveled throughout Virginia, giving 325 lectures, hosting 425 meetings, and amassing upwards of 9,200 personal contacts. Carson's prospects got a boost with the election of Franklin Delano Roosevelt and the rise of the "New Deal." A major part of the New Deal was the creation of the Civilian Conservation Corps, also known as the CCC. The CCC put legions of unemployed men back to work, usually on public land, where CCC camps sprung up and crews built dams, roads and other structure.

When President Roosevelt visited Virginia just after the formation of the CCC, he asked Mr. Carson about his thoughts on the newly developed program. Mr. Carson took full advantage of this moment and outlined his idea of a statewide park system. Mr. Roosevelt replied, "I will give you the men and the money for your state parks, if you can provide the land and will demonstrate in Virginia what such a system of parks would mean to a state."

Hungry Mother Unfolds

One park was proposed at Lake Forest in Marion, Virginia. Locals embraced the idea, even amid the throes of the economic downturn. The State Corporation Commission granted a charter to Lake Forest, Inc., on October 12 of 1929 for the purpose of providing recreation and amusement to the public.

Locals by the names of E.P. Ellis, Frank Copenhaver and Dr. J.D. Buchanan were the directors of this new corporation; its mission was to oversee a small swimming lake and a diving platform as well as a bathhouse, a dance hall, a restaurant, a picnic ground and a sizable parking area.

As reported in *The Marion Democrat* on June 3, 1930:

> The opening of Lake Forest means that for the first time the people of Marion and this section of Virginia will have a truly adequate place to swim, protected against all hazards, and in pure mountain spring water which has been declared absolutely safe by a representative of the state board of health. Lake Forest is also the first public picnic ground, especially designed for that purpose in this section, and is also the first recreation center which is devoted to the entertainment of the entire family, young and old.

This family haven only operated for three years, but it soon became part of the state park system. With much fanfare, Virginia simultaneously opened six parks on the same day, June 15, 1936, heralding a new national era in outdoor recreation. Out of the six parks, Hungry Mother was the chosen site for two days' worth of festivities. Governor George C. Peery, along with a host of local and state dignitaries, traversed miles of rocky roads to be present for the event.

The Odd Name

Hungry Mother State Park was officially announced as Southwest Virginia State Park, but somehow the original name stuck, despite the protests of the local citizenry.

Author Mack H. Sturgill has painstakingly detailed the history and development of Hungry Mother State Park. After considerable research, Mr. Sturgill is of the belief that the park name was a publicity stunt created by slightly inebriated men who devised a public relations campaign to enhance the local economy. In Sturgill's words, "The naming of the park and the accompanying legend seems to be a case of putting an old tale in a new bottle with a provocative label."

Marketing ploy or not, the famed name (and its corresponding legend) still lives on today.

MYSTERIES THEN AND NOW

Visitors to the park occasionally report hearing lonesome wails rolling across the lake at the park—and some believe they come from the spirits of the dying mother or the surviving child. Others, having heard the same strange noises, dismiss the haunted howls as the nighttime cries of the common loon. One thing is certain: mystical, melancholy cries still echo throughout Holston Valley, causing folks to scratch their heads and wonder.

EVIL OUTSIDE CABIN 13

One particular area at Hungry Mother State Park is known for its strange happenings. Cabin 13 isn't far from the site where a menace to society—a child molester—took his own life. On the run from Missouri, this man somehow landed in the sleepy, close-knit mountain valley that is Smyth County.

Knowing law enforcement from coast to coast was hunting him, the criminal abandoned his vehicle along Interstate 81 and headed to the hills just above Hungry Mother State Park. It became clear he wasn't just a predator, but a survivalist as well, because he managed to survive in the forest undetected, despite searches by state, local and park police. Days passed and the manhunt waned. Most people thought he must have escaped to another area, but that wasn't actually the case! Instead, he fashioned a hideout in a small hillside depression just above Lake Trail.

John Taminger and former park manager Jim Kelly are familiar with how the rest of the story unfolded. They say months and months passed with no sign of the criminal. It wasn't until a hiker neared the water's edge along Lake Trail when he came across a most unusual sight. At first he wasn't too sure what he saw, but he soon realized it was a human head. Terrified, he quickly found a park ranger. Park police called in the local authorities, who promptly launched a search in the depths of Hungry Mother Lake, finding nothing. Authorities then set their sights on the hills. Here, they found the decayed remains of a partial corpse.

A handgun and a suicide note were near the remains. How the head became detached from the body is a mystery.

Even though the discovery of the head was at water's edge, it is Cabin 13 where guests report mysterious encounters. Some report cloven hoof prints just outside their door. Others report glowing, vacant eyes glaring out from behind tree trunks. Such accounts are found in occasional entries in the park's cabin journals. Interestingly, the reports never come in at night; that's when the supposed creature lies in wait for its next victim.

Guests of Cabin 13 also report waking in the middle of the night and experiencing limb paralysis. Awakened for no apparent reason, they discover their muscles stiff and unable to move, while getting the feeling of a malevolent presence in the room. This weird phenomenon is known to extend several minutes leaving guests distressed. As quickly as the paralysis set in, it is gone, leaving the person thinking they hallucinated the experience.

Some park staff believe the sightings and tales are nothing more than a good old-fashioned campfire story. Others aren't so sure, believing visitors have perhaps spotted the survivalist's spirit trying to locate the rest of his body.

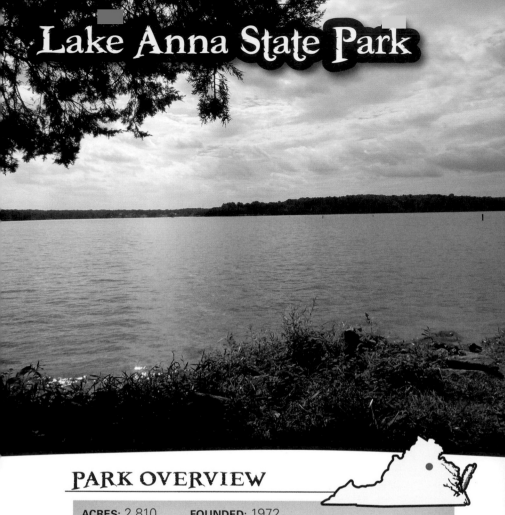

Lake Anna State Park

PARK OVERVIEW

ACRES: 2,810   **FOUNDED:** 1972

NEARBY: North Anna Nuclear Information Center, Lake Anna Winery, Historic Downtown Fredericksburg, Chancellorsville Battlefield and Visitor Center, Fredericksburg and Spotsylvania County National Military Park, Fredericksburg Area Museum and Cultural Center, Fredericksburg Battlefield Visitor Center, Fredericksburg Confederate Cemetery

NOTABLE VISITORS: Many members of the state government

ABOUT THE PARK

A Perfect Park Setting

Once the site of 18,000 acres of farmland spanning three counties, today Lake Anna State Park is best known for its pristine shorelines and boasts some of Virginia's lushest protected landscapes. Lake Anna was formed from the North Anna and Pumunkey Rivers to provide clean water to cool two nuclear power plants at the North Anna Generating Station. The 13,000-acre lake sits 72 miles south of Washington DC and is a verdant oasis that boasts a large, sandy taupe-glazed beach and 10 miles of lake frontage.

A modern cabin complex, expansive campgrounds, lakeside picnic shelters, and 15 miles of multi-use trails are a backdrop to the visitor center that was recently renovated and now features high-tech exhibits.

PARK HISTORY

A Complicated Past

Lake Anna State Park has an intriguing history. It was home to the Glenora Plantation, which is now largely demolished. The area was also home to rambunctious gold miners who sought gold nearby. Then there are the abandoned graveyards that seem constantly covered in overgrowth, despite the best efforts of park volunteers. With such a long, often dark history, one has to wonder what lies beneath the now peaceful earth where campers, swimmers, hikers and fishermen seem unfazed by the park's past.

A Gem from the Beginning

Native Americans lived along the North and South Anna Rivers and the Pigeon Run Stream for centuries. The stream got its name thanks to the many Passenger Pigeons that once inhabited the area. At some point in history, the word "stream" was dropped from Pigeon Run's name. While much of the area is now underwater in Lake Anna, remnants of its history remain visible at the park.

The park is home to the ruins of the Pigeon Run Plantation. A 3,000-acre enterprise built in the 1830s, the plantation's name was changed to Glenora following the Civil War. The name likely was a reference to the lush, emerald green glens and valleys along the stream, an appropriate name then and today.

Built in 1832 by Scotsman John Jerdone, the plantation was an affirmation of affluence and included a dairy, slave quarters, an outdoor kitchen, a bath and washhouse, a laundry and soap-making building, a smokehouse, a well house, a privy, an icehouse, and of course, the impressive manor house. John was the grandson of Francis Jerdone, a merchant who arrived in the Colonies in 1749. It is said Frank Jerdone was the first "chain store" owner in Virginia. The family was quite prosperous; the Jerdone family was associated with a number of large plantations.

Glenora Plantation was popular with the many wealthy southern aristocrats who gathered and socialized there on the way to and from Richmond and Washington DC. The house boasted marble mantels, heartwood pine floors, and superbly hand-carved wood embellishments and was enveloped within an oak-hickory forest and punctuated with sweet gum and sassafras. But when rumors of a war circulated, John Jerdone sold the manor house, outbuildings, and adjoining 3,000 acres in 1860. The land then passed from owner to owner until the 1970s when it came under the ownership of the Commonwealth of Virginia. All that remains of the original plantation is its smokehouse, making the tiny building merely a shadow of the past.

Golden Era

The park's land was home to a gold mining operation called the Goodwin Mine. Primitive records indicate Thomas

Jefferson first wrote about Virginia gold along the banks of the Rappahannock River as early as the 1750s, sparking a boom in the Commonwealth. Virginia soon became a leading producer, with approximately 250 mines in the Commonwealth. By the 1800s, hundreds of gold mines were operating in the eastern United States with nearly two dozen in Spotsylvania County, home of Lake Anna State Park. Virginia produced almost 100,000 troy ounces over nearly 150 years of gold mining. While that is impressive, it doesn't hold a candle to the amounts mined during the California gold rush.

According to historian Ben Swenson,

> Virginia's 250-odd mines permanently altered the landscape. A narrow band of abandoned pits and piles sweeps diagonally across the Commonwealth. All but a handful of these are on private property, and owners are understandably reluctant to grant access to them, because miners dug shafts to get at veins deep underground and because modern-day explorers sometimes cart off tailings (leftover rocks) in the not-unfounded belief that there still might be small amounts of gold in the spent pay dirt. Other foragers have been known to grab the scant relics remaining on these sites. Industrialist Henry Ford took souvenirs legally because he could afford to; he once bought an entire Virginia gold mine just so he could salvage the rusted and overgrown steam engine there. Despite the veil of secrecy that shrouds these sites, there is still a spot or two left where you can see what Virginia miners left behind.

The snaking drive to Lake Anna State Park is flecked with evidence of central Virginia's shining past, including Gold

Dale Road and Mine Run Grocery Store. Before there was a state park on the banks of the lake, before there was any lake at all, Spotsylvania County was the heart of Virginia's gold country.

Gold had been discovered along Pigeon Run as early as the 1820s. The vein was worked for nearly 60 years, with some success. The site was impressive in its day and the impact is still visible today. One can easily see the narrow trenches dug for diverting the flow from Pigeon Run, ensuring that a constant stream of water washed through the long sluice-boxes miners created to trap the heavy gold. The park features a self-guided interpretive trail that tells the mine's history and points out the remains of what was once an impressive operation. The visitor center is home to a model of the "rockers" or "long tom," a mechanism that helped

separate gold from the host material. According to Swenson, "the gold-bearing quartz that miners took from the ground was crushed in a stamp mill—a machine with coffee can-sized pistons powered by a steam engine that hammered the rock to a powdery consistency. Workers then mixed the ore with water and passed it over mercury-coated plates. The quartz and other minerals washed away. The gold stuck." According to Swenson, "the heat evaporated the mercury, leaving the gold behind."

A noted toxin, mercury exposure can lead to significant health problems. When you add in the dangerous machines and workings of the mine itself—the boilers, engine house, jaw crusher, stamp mill, and furnace—the mine must have been an incredibly dangerous place to work.

In fact, carboys—large glass jugs that once held the mercury itself—are still visible at the site. Swenson surmises that "all the excavation, the chemicals, must have been a nightmare for the local environment." Additionally, the toll on human life must have been horrific as well. Given the paucity of records, a definitive death toll is impossible to come by. The graveyards themselves are of little help, too. The few graves within the park's boundaries are mostly marked by large fieldstone and in some cases smaller footstones. Very little is known of individual miners and their fates.

A Sketchy Past

Historically, mining ventures have often been marked by lawlessness, and Goodwin Mine was no exception. Violence and crime were common. Swenson notes, "There must have been a constant wave of second guessing, of cold distrust: if only we had blasted the tunnel a few feet further . . . dug here instead of there. In 1870 a couple of Philadelphians were working the Goodwin Mine and came upon an especially rich vein. They set a trio of men to guard the find overnight, only to discover two of them raising the deposit in the morning. The gunshots of the loyal sentry were able to run the scofflaws off."

GOODWIN MINE ROBBERY

Known as "Gold Hill," Goodwin Gold Mine reached its peak by the late 1800s. The whole area was overtaken by gold fever. This was the case in April 1879 after the discovery of a vein of nearly solid gold along the banks of Pigeon Run.

The local paper, the *Fredericksburg Ledger*, stated, "it only took a few minutes to take out several hundred dollars" from the ground, so the miners had to take precautions. Ted Kamieniak notes in his book, *Fredericksburg, Virginia: Eclectic Histories for the Curious Reader*, "On leaving the property for the night they left a guard of three men with loaded guns, to protect the gold that was still in sight. About nine o'clock the next morning, a Sunday, two workmen from the mine were discovered to have sneaked in, and were caught collecting gold from the vein. They were ordered immediately out by the guard who had come suddenly upon them, and not going soon enough, the loyal guard fired upon them three times." The two escaped unharmed, and immediately warrants were placed for their apprehension.

The public record is silent about how this armed robbery ended. Did bounty hunters track them down, steal the gold and throw their bodies down the dark 95-foot-deep shafts? Are we even sure the mine owners told the truth and bandits and robbers escaped unharmed? Or did they merely apprehend the bandits and turn them over to local authorities? No one knows.

REMNANTS OF GOODWIN GOLD MINE

The former mine site is now in ruins. Overgrown, collapsing and now a safety hazard if you attempt to venture into it, it's still an interesting site to visit. If you look closely, you can still see the impressions where placer and shaft mining took place. Much of the site is off-limits unless you're on a scheduled tour, and for good reason: the site is full of gaping caverns and crevices. One does not need an overactive imagination to hear the sounds of machinery clanging, hissing steam boilers, straining mules, rocks tumbling down wooden chutes, and even distant screams of angry men. It's also easy to imagine the human toll from the poor ventilation and total lack of proper protective equipment, an environment where the workers were exposed to mercury poisoning every day.

CONTRARY CREEK

Contrary Creek was once a beautiful, slender tributary of the North Anna River. Today, it's a barren wasteland because of the pollution left behind by mining in the area.

When it was first mined, the land contained a variety of minerals, including gold, pyrite, zinc, copper and iron. Unfortunately, mining rocks can produce byproducts that interfere with aquatic habitats and sterilize productive ecosystems. The end result? A stream where insects, fish and mollusks are absent.

Despite numerous remediation efforts, decontamination has been unsuccessful, leaving behind a poisoned, barren landscape. Without question, this pollution led to human and environmental tragedies taking place at this site. Today, we know long-term mercury exposure can lead to sudden anger, memory loss, sleep deprivation, loss of self-control, and much more. As countless shafts and ruins run along Contrary Creek, might not a ghost be lingering amid the ruins?

GHOST ANIMAL

Contrary Creek is not exactly the most popular destination. Fishermen, hunters and even hikers don't care to explore the area. A few people have done so out of curiosity, but they invariably say it is doubtful they'll ever return. Not only is the area in and around the stream dead, but visitors describe it as incredibly eerie, a place where you can't shake the feeling that you're being watched by someone or something.

One visitor to the area saw something he couldn't explain, something straight out of the 1933 movie *The Invisible Man*. In the movie, Dr. Jack Griffin, turns invisible, leaving behind only weighted footprint impressions as he walks. That's almost exactly what the observer reported.

Others report similar experiences, such as the feeling that they were brushed up against suddenly, and it's always clear they are jolted by the experience, hesitating to share more.

Could the ghostly encounter be caused by a phantom animal? A deer that found itself at the bottom of a mine shaft with no way out? Or perhaps an animal that ingested the many poisons of Contrary Creek? It's not clear, but something is definitely out there.

MANY GRAVEYARDS

Lake Anna is home to at least three known graveyards —the Ware Cemetery, the Old Taylor Property and the Wingfield Cemetery.

Lake Anna State Park is not far from Richmond, Virginia, and one of the most famous and haunted cemeteries in America, Hollywood Cemetery. It is extraordinarily beautiful but exceedingly spooky. Its also home to notable monuments, including a 90-foot granite pyramid commemorating the deaths of 18,000 Confederate soldiers, who are buried on-site. The cemetery is also the final resting place of our fifth president, James Monroe, who lies within a birdcage tomb, and nearby is the grave site of our tenth president, John Tyler. Other notable graves include those of Confederate President Jefferson Davis and his many children, George Pickett, J.E.B. Stuart, several Virginia governors and two Supreme Court justices. The grand rolling landscape overlooks the historic James River, while an impressive collection of heritage roses and over thirty remarkable trees are interspersed within the memorial garden. But perhaps most notable, at least among those in the parapsychology community, is the well-known spiritual phenomena occurring behind the massive black gates.

Soldiers commemorated at the impressive Hollywood pyramid are said to moan and somehow reach beyond the grave, making one corner of the structure absolutely frigid. Then there are the tales told about the cemetery's sculpture of a cast iron dog. Faithfully watching over the grave of a young girl, it is said the canine occasionally moves. The area is also the site of sightings of a wispy object, believed to be the spirit of the young girl, which floats casually around the dog's foreboding body.

Another reputed haunting at the cemetery also involves dogs. Author Ellen Glasgow was buried with her two dogs at her side, and visitors report hearing, but never seeing, dogs scampering through the cemetery. Strangely, the summertime playgrounds for Ellen Glasgow were the Jerdone Plantations. If Ms. Glasgow and her two dogs frolic about Hollywood Cemetery, who is to say the threesome don't make an annual summertime trek to the grounds of Lake Anna, perhaps visiting familiar faces from long ago?

WARE CEMETERY

Lake Anna's cemeteries are reputed to be haunted as well. The former Ware property offers some of the most scenic views of Lake Anna in the park. The area was once owned by Marvin Ware, a farmer and sawmill worker who grew corn and hay and raised beef cattle. Very much a conservationist, Mr. Ware was hopeful the Commonwealth of Virginia would purchase his land, and they did in 2006, adding approximately 400 acres to Lake Anna State Park. The site is mostly forested; the cemetery is located in an undulating meadow between Ware and Pumunkey Creeks.

Ruth Ware Le Barron, Marvin's daughter, is assisting park personnel with Ware family history, since the family's graveyard now lies within the park boundary. Grave markers dating back to as early as 1848 are present and hold a commanding lookout over Lake Anna.

As much as park personnel enjoy the privilege of maintaining this location, they report seeing a shadowy figure slip between the gravestones. When I visited the park, I set out to find "the shadow." Once at the site, it didn't take long for the unexpected to happen. I was immediately overcome with an ominous feeling and it felt certain that I wasn't alone, even though I clearly was. I looked around as the sun began to set, casting long angled shadows beside the gravestones. The growing shadows heightened my fear and apprehension, and I quickly decided it was best to leave. After I shared details of my experience, I found out I wasn't the only one to have had a disconcerting experience at the cemetery. Many park employees have reported something similar.

TAYLOR RUINS

The Taylor Family cemetery is less prominent, found footsteps off a wooded pathway. At present, little is known about William Taylor, who built his family home (which also has an adjoining cemetery) in the late nineteenth century. Records date his purchase to 1879, when he obtained 100 acres for a mere $250. A year later, the 1880 census lists William and wife Rachel, along with six of their children, living on-site. (Tragically, that's several fewer children than listed in Taylor's family in the 1870 census.)

A scant trace of this family's homestead can be seen after a short woodland walk. Their home was tiny, but it was apparently peaceful. But it's not clear that it's so peaceful today. Visitors tell tales about untimely and unexplainable events: wildly falling acorns, tree bark peeling on its own accord, all for no apparent reason. Is this a remnant of the Taylor family, perhaps one of their children who died too young? No one knows.

A CONFEDERATE AND HIS FAMILY

High on a hillside overlooking Lake Anna is an enclosed cemetery holding the gravesite of Thomas Jefferson Wingfield, a Confederate soldier. Born April 14, 1832, he was raised on a farm that was on park grounds. A cavalry soldier who also served with an artillery regiment, roll call records indicate "present" on each roll call from November 1863 to April 18, 1864.

Interestingly, the war must have taken a toll; the next record of Thomas Jefferson Wingfield is one for desertion. He is listed as a "deserter" in records from Albemarle County, Virginia, dated March 24, 1865, and he received parole in Charlottesville on May 18, 1865. Despite his desertion, records indicate he joined the "William Kean Camp" of Confederate Veterans and lived a long life, dying in 1923 at the age of 91. Over time, the Wingfield family lived in several different houses on park grounds, but today, the houses are ruins, and only Wingfield's lone gravesite remains intact.

DISTANT DISTURBANCES

With so many cemeteries and such a colorful history, it's no surprise Lake Anna is a supernatural hot spot. What's more, we only know about marked graves, and it's likely there are many unmarked graves scattered throughout the park.

Perhaps such graves give rise to the mysterious phenomena reported at each cemetery: bark, acorns and dirt seem to be thrust through the air at occasional visitors. But this isn't just some child's prank; this has been reported even when the wind and wildlife are silent, and even at cemeteries where trees are uncommon.

If the stories are true, perhaps it's evidence of a poltergeist. The word originates from German; *poltern* means to "cause a racket" and geist means *ghost*. Poltergeists typically are attracted to a person who is especially troubled or one who harbors intense unhappiness, insecurity or intense aggression. Conceivably all of these emotions could have been present among the land's early residents and workers. Poltergeists can also bind themselves to places, causing havoc and chaos to whomever visits. The many accounts from bewildered park visitors certainly seem to fit this description.

Mason Neck State Park

PARK OVERVIEW

ACRES: 1,825   **FOUNDED:** 1985

NEARBY: Gunston Hall, Mount Vernon, Pohick Bay Regional Park, Woodlawn Plantation, Mason Neck National Wildlife Refuge, Meadowwood Special Recreation Area

NOTABLE VISITORS: George Mason IV, Governor Terry McAuliffe and First Lady Dorothy McAuliffe

ABOUT THE PARK

Just a half-hour drive south of Washington DC and less than 8 minutes off I-95, Mason Neck, a day-use park, is home to 1,800 acres of land and full of hiking and biking trails. Relaxation comes easy at Mason Neck, in large part because of its cool, shaded forests and its abundant wildlife that thrive amid the park's wetlands, forest, open water, ponds and open fields. The park is particularly popular with birdwatchers, who come to view the thousands of ducks found in the park. Additionally, the park is known nationally (and even internationally) for its bald eagle and tundra swan populations. The park's visitor center, renovated in 2014, features high-tech exhibits geared toward birders, including a life-sized eagle nest. Better yet, with easy access to Belmont Bay, Kanes Creek and the Potomac River, it is an excellent outdoor classroom for environmental literacy and learning. The park is also adjacent to a National Wildlife Refuge that bears the same name and which covers over 2,000 acres.

PARK HISTORY

Saving Mason Neck

You probably have heard about Rachel Carson, Aldo Leopold and Teddy Roosevelt, all great American conservationists. But have you heard of Liz Hartwell? Liz was a housewife, a mother and a garden club member when she and her family moved to the Mason Neck area of Fairfax County. "The Neck" was famous as home of the famed Mason family, including George Mason, one of the nation's Founding Fathers. An inscription in stone at the George Mason Memorial sums up Liz Hartwell's passion and activism on behalf of the natural area around her home: "Men and nature must work hand in hand. The throwing out of balance of the resources of nature throws out of balance also the lives of men."

Thanks to her efforts and those of friends and fellow travelers, much of the mature hardwoods and Potomac River shoreline at Mason Neck State Park and the Elizabeth

Hartwell National Wildlife Refuge has been preserved. Hartwell is credited with saving much of The Neck from developers. She, along with a host of other influential local individuals, led a campaign to save over 5,000 acres from a proposed mixed-use development. Their battle was difficult, but ultimately the park supporters were victorious. The victory has proved important, as the area has proved crucial to the resurgence in the American bald eagle population.

JITTERS AT THE JAMMES HOUSE

Perched about 20 feet above the Potomac River, a white two-story clapboard house with a detached greenhouse clings to the cliffs of Mason Neck State Park. It's a home many couples only dream about. Unfortunately, its inhabitants only got to enjoy living there for a short time. The occupants were Doctor Jammes, his wife and two daughters.

Disaster struck when the couple were in their 40s. They had left their young daughters in the care of a grandmother and traveled to Yellowstone National Park for a winter holiday. While there, they rented snowmobiles and were traveling along one of the park's outstanding trails when they had a horrific accident. In an instant, their lives were snuffed out and their daughters orphaned.

Once their estate was settled, the Department of Conservation and Recreation purchased the property. Sitting on a grassy knoll, the beautifully manicured residence is situated in an absolutely serene setting.

But visits to the house are anything but pleasant. Visitors become uneasy immediately upon entering the foyer. Today the site is used as a meeting house and for overnight accommodations for volunteers and staff. Almost invariably, haunting stories are passed along, and only a brief mention of such tales is needed to spur others to contribute their firsthand accounts.

Like most old homes, the Jammes House has its own creaks and bumps and a host of unexplained noises. Punishing winds whip across the bay, causing bone-chilling drafts to blast through the rooms. A loosely latched screen door repeatedly swings open only to slam shut with the next passing gust.

That's another complaint: the home is consistently cold, no matter the season or the time of day. Some attribute this to atmospheric pressure or simple nerves, and to be sure, not everyone who enters the Jammes House agrees that something sinister lurks about.

However, many staff members and visitors talk of the daunting feeling they get when passing through the scores of empty rooms. In particular, the home's bathrooms seem haunted, and the house has many bathrooms. And despite the cheery, 1960s-era decor, most visitors report that the site is inhabited by a peculiar presence. Guests remark they have sensed someone watching them walk through the house but find no one when looking up. The experiences are so heartfelt and told with such obvious strain that they sound like something straight out of a horror film. Witnesses all agree: they never intend to spend a night alone in the house. However, some must as part of their job. Paula Hill, Executive Assistant for state parks, reports that one assignment required that she spend the night in reportedly the most haunted bedroom in the house. A bit frightened, she retired and slipped between the chilly sheets. The room was pitch dark and silent. Suddenly, she felt a soft swoosh, and something rushed from one side of the room to the other. Hill tensed with fear, and again, a second swoosh went bouncing from wall to wall. Frightened, she inched deeper under the covers, anxiously awaiting sunrise.

The top of the stairs are another hot spot of paranormal activity. When visitors reach the top of the stairs, they are often flooded with thoughts of an ominous presence and images of a little dead girl.

Things get really eerie when you open the short door to the left of the staircase. When you open the door, it leads to a solid wall. This is one of the strangest sights in the Jammes House. So why was it built? One explanation is that it was specifically built with spirits in mind; it was thought that it would confuse the spirits and drive them from the residence. Obviously, that tactic is not foolproof, given the multitude of paranormal stories shared about the site.

Directly opposite the staircase is what some believe to be one of the most haunted places in the entire house: a tiny pink bathroom. Many refuse to enter this deceptively cheery room, believing a ghost hides behind the shower curtain and is lying in wait for its next victim. The visitors who dare to enter report an oppressive, claustrophobic feeling, a room that is dungeon-like despite its rosy decor.

A few individuals think the ghost residing on the building's second story belongs to the little girl whose picture hangs in the first-floor master suite. Approximately seven or eight years of age, she was one of the Jammes' daughters. But here's the odd thing: she's still alive. One wonders if perhaps the ghost was one of her playmates or someone else she associated with in childhood.

The Jammes House is infamous for another reason: items disappear. One such instance involved a disappearing bowl. Along with another staff member, I was preparing refreshments for some of our nation's state park leaders, who were visiting the park. We noticed one of the faux crystal bowls was missing. After looking in all the usual places and in some unusual places, we still couldn't find it. Twenty-four hours passed and still no one had seen the bowl. Feeling certain it was the handiwork of the young ghost from the second-story wing, I took several steps up the back stairs and looked in the direction of the small bedroom and said, "Give us our bowl back." Nothing. I demanded its return a second time, at which point I felt a very cold presence, and suddenly got the impression that the bowl was in a dresser drawer. Within moments, another park employee entered the kitchen. Without explaining, we asked if he would mind looking for the bowl in the upstairs dresser drawer. Looking at the two of us with an odd expression, he proceeded up the rear staircase in search of the faux crystal. When I turned around, the bowl was in front of me. I looked at the staff member next to me, and we both erupted into shrill laughter. What really happened? Was it a ghost or an eruption of some sort of psycho-kinetic energy? Or were our minds just creating what we longed to see?

To this day, disturbances still erupt at the Jammes House, so there is little doubt that not everything about this pristine hideaway is tangible and corporeal.

Natural Tunnel State Park

PARK OVERVIEW

ACRES: 950   **FOUNDED:** 1971

NEARBY: Scott County Park, Carter's Fold, Cumberland Gap National Historical Park, Wilderness Road State Park, Southwest Virginia Historical Museum, Bristol International Raceway, The Crooked Road, Virginia Heritage Music Trail

NOTABLE VISITORS: William Jennings Bryan, Teddy Roosevelt, Eleanor Roosevelt, Governor Abner Linwood Holton Jr.

ABOUT THE PARK

Embracing the Landscape

In 1967 the state acquired about 140 acres from the Natural Tunnel Chasm and Caverns Corporation, which had operated the famous Natural Tunnel tourism attraction that included a lodge, a restaurant, a gift shop, a picnic area and trails. In May of 1971 the state park officially opened. The main attraction is Natural Tunnel itself, an 850-foot-long tunnel carved out by Stock Creek over millions of years. It has been said that William Jennings Bryan once dubbed it "the Eighth Wonder of the World." Promoters have been using that quote to promote tourism to the area for more than 100 years.

Approximately 750 additional acres were acquired later, and the park's campground opened in 1974. In the last decade, the park added new RV campsites, along with ten cabins, a family lodge, and an environmental education and conference center. A variety of trails, a swimming pool with a 100-foot slide, and a chairlift to the tunnel floor are located at the park. One of the main attractions is the replica Anderson Blockhouse, a pioneer-era fort built by the Daniel Boone Wilderness Trail Association in 2003.

PARK HISTORY

The area's American Indians were the first people to see Natural Tunnel, and the first person of European descent to view the geological wonder was likely Daniel Boone, who saw the site in 1775 on his trip on the Wilderness Road to Kentucky. The first recorded mention of Natural Tunnel is traced to Francis Walker Gilmer, a student of Thomas Jefferson, who wrote a paper in 1816 entitled, "On the Geological Formation of the Natural Bridge of Virginia." He compared Natural Tunnel to the more well-known Natural Bridge located in Rockbridge County, Virginia. One of the earliest reports of Natural Tunnel as a tourist attraction comes from C.F.M. Garnett, who in 1853 notes, "The natural tunnel in Scott County and the large and beautiful cave in the same neighborhood are considerations which would alone attract crowds of visitors . . ." By 1859, the Tunnel was resurveyed as a possible site of a railroad bed, however, the Civil War brought about a halt to nearly all commerce in the South. Eventually, a pair of railroad lines were built in the tunnel, and they carried passengers and cargo. The last passengers passed through the tunnel in 1939.

The tunnel wasn't just home to a railroad; former president Theodore Roosevelt also visited the area sometime around the turn of the twentieth century. A picture of a large group of individuals hangs in the park's visitor center; the group had climbed up the steep side of the tunnel to have a photo taken. A handwritten note on the photograph reads, "Theodore Roosevelt and party."

Burning of Cove Ridge Center

In 1992, a multi-purpose environmental education center was approved for Natural Tunnel State Park. An impressive structure, plans called for a meeting space, classrooms and a dormitory-style residence hall.

Soon thereafter, construction began, and it was nearly complete when disaster struck and the center burst into flames. No one knows exactly how the building burned down, but some staff suggest a lonesome spirit was to blame.

Thankfully, Cove Ridge Center, as it is now known, was rebuilt, and it's a source of community pride and a favorite meeting place for park visitors, as well as a popular site for family reunions and outdoor recreation and environmental classes.

THE GHOST OF COVE RIDGE

Apparently, the park's visitors weren't the only ones who celebrated when the Cove Ridge Center was rebuilt. A ghost enjoys inhabiting the structure as well. Affectionately referred to as "Wallace," the ghost does not appear in the form of a full-bodied apparition or a mysterious orb, but simply as a noisemaker. It seems Wallace has an affinity for rambling about this large open-air modern mountain structure. Staffers have any number of ideas about why Wallace is present. Some say he may be looking for his final resting place, while others argue he's trying to solve the arson of the first Cove Ridge Center. Perhaps he's trying to reach beneath the wooden floorboards in search of the land that was once his homestead.

Whatever the reason, "Wallace is there" is a common refrain. One staff member shares a spooky encounter. She was in the kitchen when she heard someone say "hello." This perplexed her, as she was alone in the building. This immediately made her remember the many occasions when she heard unexplained noises in the building. Mentioning the strange event to a park ranger on duty, the officer investigated, only to find the building completely secured with no sign of any unlawful intrusion. Since then, this has happened time and again, and staff are now accustomed to Wallace's company and believe him to be a harmless, if eerie, companion from long ago.

LOVERS' LEAP

According to a legend dating back to the late nineteenth century, a pair of American Indian lovers leapt to their deaths off the steep, towering granite cliffs above Stock Creek. The inseparable lovers were from two different tribes, one Cherokee and the other Shawnee. Differences among the tribal leaders prohibited them from marrying, so they did the unthinkable and jumped into the abyss.

A short trail (less than a half mile) memorializes the legend and follows the rim of the deep gorge; on the trail, visitors can get a closer look at the legend's site. Thankfully, a chain-link fence protects visitors from the 450-foot fall.

Given the site's tragic history, it's not surprising that ghost stories continue to circulate. Sightings are most often reported on gloomy nights when thick, clammy fog hugs the gray granite, and staff members report spotting the outline of the two young lovers on the cliff's edge and hearing their whispered voices ricochet off the rock walls.

Contemporary legend offers more detail: the two are reported to embrace before spilling downward into the mist. According to eyewitnesses, the two figures never scream in terror; instead, they simply fall, perhaps reliving their last few moments on earth before tumbling back into the afterlife.

CAMPGROUND CEMETERY

Megan Krager, the park interpreter, shares a favorite story about the park, which goes something like this: There is a small cemetery in the Natural Tunnel Campground where a ghostly shadow sometimes appears. Occasionally the shadowy figure is so clear witnesses make out particular details. They describe a vaporous form with the visage of an old woman with a hateful, downturned gaze. Area residents speculate it is the soul of a local woman who was spiteful to everyone she encountered.

The woman's earthly life finally came to a close after six decades of hateful living. When it came time to bury her, family members refused to bury her near the family plots. Instead, she was buried miles away, near the park's campground. Wanting to be rid of the corpse as quickly as possible, the family dug a grave that was too shallow. It wasn't long afterward that spring rains fell, causing the soil to collapse around the cadaver, exposing the decaying remains.

When the remains were found, the bare bones of one hand were pointing heavenward, perhaps in a futile attempt to find salvation. Family members soon exhumed whatever body parts remained. As they dug and pulled at the decayed flesh and old bones, fragments yanked loose and were unceremoniously tossed into a nearby box. Finally a cavernous new grave was prepared, and the heap of remains was tossed in, striking bottom with a muffled thud. At that precise moment, an icy chill raced up the spines of the assembled family members. Reputedly, this was the exact moment when the spirit began to haunt the campground.

PARK RESIDENCE

There is another lesser-known tale about an otherworldly resident at Natural Tunnel. It seems that a spirit, possibly that of old Lucille Taylor, the former owner of a park residence, still enjoys meandering about her sprawling home. Now used to house park employees, one former resident enjoyed staying at the home, but suspects she was staying with more than her immediate family. Often she would find the door between the kitchen and storeroom open even though she had just closed it. This strange occurrence happened on a regular basis. She became so accustomed to finding it open that she accepted it as fact that she was not alone in the kitchen. Peculiarly, there was a restroom in a nearby storeroom. The wife couldn't help but wonder if its placement was a throw-back to an earlier era when Mrs. Taylor had hired help. Was this the help's lavatory? She always wondered if the hired help was working alongside her? Or maybe Lucille was rambling about enjoying the mountain views?

THE CYCLONE OF RYE COVE

One reported haunting is located just outside the park grounds and involves a tragedy that the community still remembers today. It happened on May 9, 1929. One of the most intriguing accounts of that fateful day involves two journalists from a local Richmond television station.

They were on the scene to report about what is known as the Rye Cove Cyclone. A reporter and a photographer visited 100-year-old Dorothy Elkins, who was only 15 years old when a deadly twister destroyed the local two-story schoolhouse, forever changing this quiet country town. There were 150 people in the building on that fateful day.

Elkins still had a vivid memory of that day: "I'd like to forget it," she exclaims with downturned facial features, the torment still visible some 85 years later.

"The sky grew darker and darker. The principal rang the bell five minutes early. The windows blew out first, then the top went off. I felt the walls coming in on me." Mrs. Elkins recalls being on the second floor when the building began flying apart. She watched in horror when the boy sitting next to her was thrown to one side of the building; Dorothy was flung to the other side.

The TV journalists located that boy's son, Cecil Clendene. Mr. Clendene says his father spent 30–40 days in the hospital with two broken legs and a severe concussion. Mrs. Elkins also received a blow to the head that knocked her out. When she awoke her eyes were filled with dirt but she was able to see. "All that was visible was a pile of rubble, an eruption of smoldering ruins," as she recalls.

What once was her schoolhouse was now a burning wreck, the fire started by an overturned kitchen stove. Sorrowful wails could be heard everywhere and grief-stricken parents frantically searched through the wreckage. Elkins specifically recalled a boy who was killed when his head struck a nail as the building came apart.

The Fletcher family was especially hard hit, as it lost two girls: Monnie Mary, and her seven-year-old relative, Dorothy Bernice. Emma Jean Wright, a relative of the deceased, shared a telling detail with the journalists: the two girls shared one coffin.

Immediately after the disaster, rescue was difficult because the community was isolated and few people owned cars. The injured were placed on stretchers and eventually transported by rail down the mountain into Bristol. Ms. Elkins recalls "it was slow going." Today, a log cabin used by the Red Cross also doubles as a museum to the catastrophe.

A.P. Carter, a member of Virginia's renowned Carter Family, was in the next valley over but ended up being one of the first rescuers on the scene. He memorialized that tragedy in a song titled "The Cyclone of Rye Cove." The haunting lyrics tell of the horrors of that fateful day in 1929:

> Rye Cove, Rye Cove
> the place of my childhood and home, it's so silent
> and lone
> the lightning flashed, the children all cried
> dying on a pillow of stone.

Today, a lone road marker stands outside the rebuilt schoolhouse as a somber tribute. Memories of this event still linger, and if you believe the stories, mysterious manifestations do as well.

A LOCAL'S ACCOUNT OF RYE COVE

Spirits reportedly still roam the school grounds. One common story goes something like this: After school released for the day, a classmate and a few friends hung out on school grounds. They found themselves behind the tennis courts when a little girl walked by only to drift off into thin air. Spooked out of their wits, they told their parents of this disembodied apparition. The parents told the children about the tornado disaster for the first time. The girls were visibly shaken and shrieked when they were told of the maimed, charred bodies amid the debris and the lifeless forms dangling from nearby trees.

BRICK CHURCH

Not too far down the road from the Rye Cove schoolhouse sits a quaint brick church perched on the side of a hill. About four miles from Natural Tunnel and a little less than two miles from Rye Cove, it's a fine brick building with plank flooring and a pulpit of local black walnut.

The local Horton family was hired to build the church, and when they built the structure, they used slave labor to finish the structure's stone fence. It is here that visitors report hearing low-pitched baritone voices rising and falling in an eerily similar manner to the old spirituals sung by slaves. Many presume it is the sad souls of the black men still toiling away.

NEARBY HAUNTS

Tales of phantoms and weird occurrences reach far beyond Natural Tunnel State Park, and they are found even miles down the road into Gate City. Nancy Horton, the park's office manager, shares a chilling account of an incident that took place at her parent's home not long after her grandfather's death.

One day while visiting the home she heard a strange sound in the basement. At first, she brushed it off, but the noise continued, so she stopped what she was doing and listened intently. As she mulled it over, she kept thinking that it sounded like a shovel being scraped across the basement floor, as if someone were downstairs scraping coal. Flashes of her childhood raced through her mind as she recalled the cold nights in the house that were always followed by her grandpa shoveling the last bit of coal off the floor and into the old cast iron boiler. Just after she heard the noise, she noticed the air temperature rise; then she heard footsteps climbing the cellar stairs. To her astonishment, first-floor doors started opening and closing on their own. More than a little unnerved, she told herself to take a big breath and relax. After all, grandpa was a gentle soul, and knowing he was present was really a great comfort.

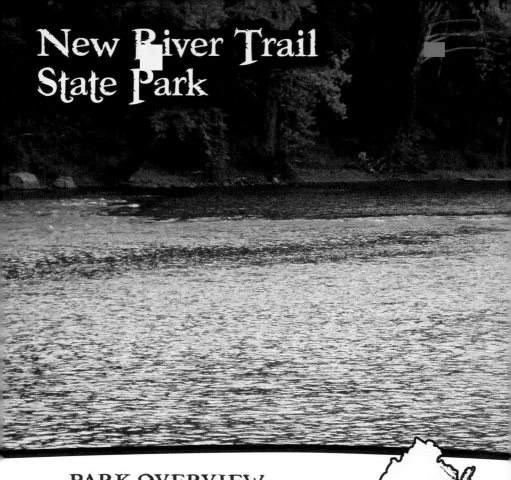

New River Trail State Park

PARK OVERVIEW

ACRES: 1,337   **FOUNDED:** 1986

AVERAGE WIDTH: 80 feet   **TOTAL LENGTH:** 57 miles

NEARBY: Historic Shot Tower, Foster Falls Historic Village, Mark E. Hufeisen Horse Complex, Dannelly Park, Draper Mercantile, Mount Rogers National Recreation Area, Big Survey Wildlife Management Area, Major Graham Mansion

NOTABLE VISITORS: U.S. Senators Mark Warner and Tim Kaine, Governor Terry McAuliffe, Thomas Lafayette Felts of the Baldwin-Felts Detective Agency, and Colonel Francis Fries

ABOUT THE PARK

New River Trail is unique among Virginia's state parks. It is 57.7 miles long and averages only 80 feet wide. It was the state's first rail-to-trail conversion, which means that the park is essentially centered upon a section of rail line that was abandoned by Norfolk Southern in the 1980s after about 100 years of service.

The park begins in the town of Pulaski and passes through Pulaski, Wythe, Carroll and Grayson Counties. After that, it splits into two parts, where Chestnut Creek flows into the New River at what is called Fries Junction. One arm ends at State Route 58 in Galax with an impressive spur that takes you past Chestnut Falls and Cliff View Station. The other arm ends in Fries, the old company town built by the Washington Mills company.

Features of the linear park include two historic tunnels, three major bridges and nearly 30 smaller bridges and trestles. Twelve access points are available, eight of them providing horse trailer parking, and two have gift shops. The trail is also home to primitive camping options, an amphitheater and a 200-year-old shot tower (which was used in the manufacture of lead shot). Equestrians can even rent horses from the Foster Falls Stables.

PARK HISTORY

The sheer beauty and the wildlife resources are the primary reasons American Indians first visited the area more than 12,000 years ago. From the fish weirs on the New River to Clovis Points found throughout the park, many archaeological relics can still be seen in the region.

European explorers first visited the area in the seventeenth century. Over time, reports from explorers filtered back to the Capitol at Williamsburg from the likes of John Chiswell, William Byrd, Daniel Boone and Joseph Martin. They promoted the westward expansion of Virginia into the region and beyond.

By the middle of the eighteenth century, the Grayson Sulphur Springs was operating as a retreat for the rich and famous, who traveled from New England and the coastal plain to this mountain resort to fish, hunt, play lawn games, soak in healing waters, breathe clean mountain air and escape the heat and stench of the cities. The resort was rebuilt several times during its existence, but it was dealt a death blow when Appalachian Power built its first hydroelectric plant at Byllesby Dam, submerging the resort beneath the waters held back by the dam.

The railroad tracks that would eventually lay the groundwork for the park were built to exploit the area's copious natural resources. There were once lead and zinc mines at Austinville, iron furnaces throughout the entire region, widespread timber and coal, not to mention a Washington Mills cotton mill in Fries and the National Carbide plant in Ivanhoe.

The area's mines, factories and plants were places of hardship for many workers. Child labor was common, and despite legislation dedicated to curbing it, it took decades for the laws to take hold. In the interim, the mills and mines took their toll, and many men, women and children were crushed, broken and killed while at work. When they weren't at work, miners and iron workers resided in the hundreds of shacks that sprawled across the hills.

Eventually, many of the natural resources in the region were tapped out; this led the factories to close and unemployment to rise.

Today, much of southwest Virginia's economy is dependent on the area's scenic beauty and its cultural resources. The area has much to offer. In addition to the state park, the region is home to the Mount Rogers National Recreation Area and the Big Survey Wildlife Management Area.

Today, the park's centerpiece and headquarters are located at Foster Falls and feature an original railroad depot, remnants of an iron furnace, a fully intact 1880s mining hotel and many other historic structures that showcase what life was like at the turn of the twentieth century.

THE "NEW" RIVER

Despite its name, The New River is the earth's second-oldest river, and generations of locals and now newcomers alike affectionately refer to the north-flowing waterway simply as "The New." Perhaps it's the river's antiquity, but the site is a hot spot of unexplained encounters. In the words of local author Ronald R. Delby, "New River is eerie, especially when the fog comes out of the waters. When camping there, the fog sometimes appears as figures standing on the water." Maybe it's just the fog that gives rise to so many stories, or maybe there is something really there.

GHOSTLY MOUNTAIN LIGHTS

Each year over a million visitors delight in hiking, biking or horseback riding amid the limestone cliffs that flank much of the trail. The trail is well shaded and remarkably quiet (a rarity in an era when nearly everything makes noise). Overall, a peace and quiet dominates, but the park can also be more than a little eerie.

A RAILROAD ACCIDENT

Few railroads avoided accidents, and that was certainly true of the line present here as well. The most significant accident occurred when two local trains collided—one a passenger train, and the other carrying cargo. It all happened on November 16, 1928, on the outskirts of a small village called Fries, and the crash resulted in many injuries and three deaths.

The victims were simply in the wrong place at the wrong time. One was an employee of the railway and the other two, railway customers. All three were riding Passenger Train No. 57 when a freight engine sped toward Fries Junction hoping to beat the passenger train to the switch. As it careened around the curve it plowed through the passenger coach splitting it in half.

According to local reports, three individuals died from the overwhelming heat of the steam escaping from the ruined boiler. Lee Manuel, 39, of Pulaski, was employed as the passenger train brakeman; William Dillon and Gladys Carpenter both were locals riding the passenger train.

The local *Gazette* reported that the deceased brakeman left for work the morning of the wreck after telling his wife a dream he'd had about a deadly train wreck. Eerily, the *Gazette* reported that an agent of the Norfolk and Western had experienced the same dream.

A HAUNTED RAILWAY?

Perhaps not coincidentally, numerous locals claim to have seen mysterious lights along the New River Trail. The ghostly tales say the weird phenomenon takes place near the precise location of the deadly train wreck from 1928. Others also claim they see the lights miles away near Ivanhoe and Austinville.

Two park rangers encountered exactly this phenomenon near the Fries Junction. The pair were engrossed in conversation about development of the then-infant park. Speaking endlessly and excitedly, they outlined the possibilities for the 57-mile multi-use trail; one can be certain the rangers were not thinking about the train wreck at Fries Junction back on Friday, November 16, 1928.

The rangers were finishing their evening patrol a short distance from Fries Junction. Under the dark sky of a new moon and the shadowy cliffs surrounding their vehicle, the men spotted a dim light in the distance about a half mile south down the track. Conversation halted. Immediately the rangers questioned each other about what they were seeing, knowing that there is hardly any semblance of a road next to the recreational trail. They confirmed with each other that they were seeing and hearing the same thing: a light about

10 feet high accompanied by the clattering of cars over train tracks. The sound appeared to be coming closer. Each man sat paralyzed in their seats as the light grew larger and the sound became louder and louder.

Shaken, the ranger driving the car swerved off of the trail, and at that moment, the apparition vanished. Both men were silent as they stared and tried to process what they had just seen. Were these the trail's mysterious lights and sounds the locals commonly mentioned? Could this have been the phantom train from the Fries Junction crash? Both rangers believe it was!

They aren't alone. Residents that live along the former track site still report seeing the bright train lights and hearing the haunting clatter of the two trains that once collided on this mountain track.

THE GHOST TRAIN SCULPTURE

At the north end of the trail, between Draper and Pulaski, the visitor will come upon a peculiar piece of art known as "the Ghost Train." It consists of five metal structures and a telescope at each end of the piece, enabling the viewer to peer though the structures. No dreadful legends are associated with the site, but a former staff member recalls a strange encounter late one evening when finishing a patrol.

Nathan Younger's daily patrol was coming to an end where he prepared himself to exit at the Pulaski trailhead. An abandoned residence is located nearby; trespassing in the house is strictly prohibited. Having passed the dilapidated house hundreds of times in the past, Ranger Younger took a passing glance when suddenly he became uneasy. The door of the two-story home was hanging wide open and a flicker of light could be seen through the broken window panes. *Trespassers*, he thought to himself, more than likely bored teenagers.

Pulling his patrol vehicle off the trail, he headed to the house and waded through the overgrowth of ferns. Tearing the cobwebs from the doorway, he peeked inside first then burst over the decayed threshold. He was surprised to find what appeared to be an empty structure. There was no light source and no sign of a candle being extinguished or the lingering aroma from a wick. Was the diminutive light a flashlight? He wasn't sure.

The longer he stayed, the more he couldn't shake the idea that he was seeing things. *Ghosts!*, he thought. The further he ventured into house, the stronger the feeling got. Adrenaline shot through his veins with each step. The house was deathly cold, much colder than outside, and some areas were far colder than others. After checking the house, the ranger relocked the house, hustled back to his vehicle and threw it into drive, leaving as quickly as the law allowed.

HEAD IN HIS HANDS

The Horse Show Grounds are one popular spot near the Ivanhoe trailhead. Walking through the Show Grounds is like stepping back in time to the 1950s; one might encounter anything from rambunctious tractor pulls to peaceful riverside equestrian camps. When I visited the Show Grounds with my husband, we noticed a man in his mid-40s perched next to the campfire, with horse still tethered at his side. The man sat holding his head in his hands, so we asked if there was anything we could do to help.

He told us he had just returned from a day's trail ride, but it wasn't an ordinary one. That's when we noticed his eyes had a wild gaze and his hands were trembling. He was quick to share his story.

It began about 5:30 a.m. and daylight was beginning to break over the mountain. He headed northbound toward Austinville on horseback. Upon his approach to the Ivanhoe Trestle, his horse gave a whinny and reared her head. Up ahead were two hovering lights that appeared to be moving closer. The horse was clearly startled, and so was he. He spoke up, hoping to avoid spooking his horse and assuming he'd get a "hello" in return, from what he assumed were hikers. As the lights inched ever closer, he spoke again, this time in a stronger, louder voice. Oddly, at this second calling, the lights dashed off the trail only to disappear out over the open field. Brushing it off as ornery teens playing with flashlights, he thought nothing more of the event until he remembered other campers sharing tales of the ghostly train lights.

The morning unfolded into an enjoyable afternoon and all was well until he headed back. A monument to the birthplace of Stephen F. Austin, known as the Father of Texas, is present at the trail's intersection with Store Hill Road. As a history aficionado, he'd always heard about the monument down by the river but never saw it up close. Today was the day he decided to see it. That decision left him unnerved for the remainder of the day and perhaps for much longer.

He had nearly reached the monument when he heard the sounds of chains rattling. With teeth clinched, he says he then saw several figures hovering above the water. If that wasn't terrifying enough, they appeared to be drifting toward him. Gripped with fear, he swiftly tugged the mare's reins, turning her back toward the trail.

Convinced he had just seen ghosts, perhaps the spirits of former slaves, he set his eyes on the trail and ultimately headed back to camp. He has not returned since.

MAJOR GRAHAM MANSION

Major David Graham, the Civil War hero, was the former owner of an imposing brick mansion in the vicinity of the park. It's also one of the more haunted structures in the area. Originally known as Cedar Run, the land was purchased by Major Graham in 1826, and a mansion slowly took shape, with the first structure erected in 1838. This building was augmented and embellished over time as the family's fortune grew.

Prior to Graham's purchase of the mountainside, a slave owner by the name of Joseph Baker owned a cabin where he kept a number of slaves. Rumors are that he was a ruthless overseer; in fact, he was so bad that two of his slaves murdered him in 1786. The two slaves, Bob and Sam, were promptly hung on the site, dying a slow, painful death.

Today, the historic mansion is owned by Josiah Cephas Weaver, a songwriter and businessman. The unique landmark holds the distinction of being on both the National Register of Historic Places and the Commonwealth's Historic Register. The impressive old mansion and its several resident ghosts are a popular tourist attraction, especially during the Halloween season.

I stumbled upon the place with my husband during the dog days of August. The mansion sits upon a hill and can be viewed from the road, but the foreboding property comes alive once one enters the massive iron gates.

For ghost hunters and historians alike, these old homes dotting America's country roads are well worth visiting. Inside we learned about a friendly ghost named Clara. She was the adopted child of Major Graham's sister, Bettie, who along with her sister, Emily, taught local children to read and write.

The day we visited had elements of ghostly activity. We made our way through the house to enter what is affectionately referred to as "Clara's Room." Here we listened as the docent spoke of Clara making an occasional appearance, and in fact she visited us that August afternoon. The docent placed a ball in the center of the bedroom while visitors lined the walls. We watched in silence for any movement; only moments later the ball began rolling toward the door and moved in a circular lap around the room. Everyone stiffened and glanced at one another to verify if what they had just seen had really happened. A few broke the silence by saying, "Clara has joined us today." Did she really, or are the floors of this centuries-old home so crooked that the docent knew exactly where to place the ball to produce the trick?

Despite its hardworking staff, the structure is dusty and dank. The grandeur of the mansion is overshadowed by scabbed, outdated wallpaper, creaky, dingy floorboards, and musty rooms that smell of decay. Without question, the dreary, brick-clad basement is creepiest of all. Here, slaves were once imprisoned and chained to the basement walls.

Upon exiting, we felt unnerved, especially given the basement's awful history. On the way back to our car, we saw what appeared to be impressions of two faces in the lawn; they seemed to emerge from the lawn, causing us both to freeze before heading ever faster to our car. Perhaps the spirits of the lynched slaves Bob and Sam still lurk on these haunted grounds.

Occoneechee State Park

PARK OVERVIEW

ACRES: 2,698   **FOUNDED:** 1968

NEARBY: Prestwood Plantation, John H. Kerr Dam and Visitor Center, Molliver Vineyards and Winery, Historic Clarksville

NOTABLE VISITORS: Governor Mills E. Godwin, Park Director Ben Bolen, Chief John Jeffries Blackfeather of the Occaneechi Tribe of the Saponi Nation

ABOUT THE PARK

Occoneechee State Park serves as the gateway to John H. Kerr Reservoir, also known as Buggs Island Lake and one of the largest bodies of water in the southeastern United States. The reservoir offers access to 48,000 acres for fishing and recreation, and the park boasts thirteen modern cabins and forty-eight campsites in addition to a modern marina, several boat launches, 20 miles of multi-use trails, an equestrian campground, and a visitor center with American Indian exhibits.

PARK HISTORY

Early Years of the Land

Occoneechee State Park was first inhabited by a number of American Indian tribes, including the Occaneechi, the Saponi and the Tutelo. These tribes took up residence on three islands in the Roanoke River, now called the Staunton River. The islands were part of a trade route that brought goods to the region. The Occoneechee lived on the largest of the three islands, which was about four miles long. One can imagine that this island was their fortress, protected by water on all sides and giving them a decided advantage over any hostile tribes. The river was also an abundant source of fish, fresh water and food.

The first reference to the area in European literature occurs in 1650, when an English explorer wrote about the "Occonacheans" who lived along the north bank of the Roanoke River. They raised a variety of crops on the land and were also involved in fur trading.

Archaeologists considered the islands to be among the richest American Indian sites in the country. A former park manager with a keen eye for artifacts assembled an impressive collection of arrow and spear points, stone axes and rock tools that are now part of the state park collection. Unfortunately, the islands were later submerged in the early 1950s, when the islands became part of Buggs Island Lake as part of a hydroelectric project. At the time, the area American Indians called the Roanoke the "river of death" because of the destruction caused by the creation of the 50,000-acre reservoir.

One particularly chilling account of the park's history comes from colonist William Byrd in his diary of 1733. He was a leader of the survey parties that drew the boundary line between Virginia and North Carolina. Along the way, they encountered a ghost town on Occoneechi Island; an Indian village with huts and longhouses still intact but devoid of human inhabitants. Speculation is that this is due to disease brought by Europeans or perhaps even outright genocide.

Skirmishes between Europeans and American Indians in the area began almost immediately after settlement. But the 1670s were an especially dark decade, as Nathaniel Bacon led a rebellion in Virginia that led to the deaths of many American Indians. Known today as Bacon's Rebellion,

Bacon believed Colonial Governor William Berkeley used his family's powerful influence in England to create a too-cozy relationship with Virginia's tobacco business. Bacon also believed Berkeley was too slow in responding to Indian attacks, so with the backing of a small band of local settlers, Bacon launched an attack on the (often friendly) natives. His hideous ambushes massacred many men, women and children and drove survivors into what is now North Carolina. Bacon's battle against the Indians was seen as a great victory, empowering him to move against the colonial governor. This led to the burning of Jamestown and the eventual recall of William Berkeley to England. Bacon's Rebellion folded after Bacon died of dysentery. Sadly, many of the American Indian tribes never recovered.

THE PLANTATION HOUSE

In 1760, Thomas Jefferson's uncle, Field Jefferson, acquired 2,200 acres of land that eventually became part of the park. In 1818, Colonel William Townes purchased what became known as the Occoneechee Plantation and began building a large house in 1839 to accommodate his family. Col. Townes became quite the entrepreneur, raising tobacco and breeding thoroughbred horses, while becoming president of the Roanoke River Colt Sales Association. During his lifetime, the Occoneechee Plantation consisted of the grand two-story structure, with additions on each end, along with numerous outbuildings. After Townes' death around 1870, the land and house were sold to a former Confederate officer, Dempsey Graves Crudup, who died in an accidental house fire in the plantation house on Christmas Eve of 1898. The fire was most likely started by candles used to decorate the family Christmas tree. He was laid to rest on the property in what some believe is a not-so-restful grave.

Today, the Old Plantation Trail passes through the stony remnants of the 20-room Occoneechee Plantation. One can easily imagine the restless spirit of Mr. Crudup lurking in the dark forested area around the plantation ruins that are now punctuated with enormous boxwoods and Osage orange trees. Reportedly, visitors hear leaves rustling even when the wind is still. Some even say that they hear a voice whimpering amid what sounds like the snapping and crackling of burning timber. A few even share that they've smelled the pungent odor of burning flesh when hiking the trail. However, despite many searches, no corresponding evidence is ever found.

MYSTERY ON THE WATER

Park visitors also often report strange wraith-like shapes moving across the waters at the state park. Some claim that these are the apparitions of ethereal spirits hovering above a flooded grave. They go on to say that the ghostly shimmerings look hazy at first sight then take on lifelike forms and shapes, particularly under the light of a full moon.

Another tale about Occoneechee Plantation is recorded by L.B. Taylor in *The Ghosts of Virginia*. Taylor's research unearthed a tale about a curse preceding colonization. For some reason or other, the Indians placed a curse on a patch of land. Nothing grows on that land; no agricultural crop, no wildflower, no weeds, nothing. Instead, visitors unanimously report an ominous feeling when visiting the site, which has rightly earned the name "Hell's Acre." This site may no longer be viewed because it lies under the watery depths of the lake.

A FIRSTHAND ENCOUNTER WITH BIGFOOT

Ghosts aren't the only paranormal sights to be seen at the park. I visited the park with husband and our dachshund in the mid 1990s; we were trekking along the Panhandle Multi-use Trail when we noticed a large creature lumbering between the tall timbers along this isolated path. We gasped and whispered excitedly and then went silent as we watched it. Even the dog was silent, which is saying something for a dachshund. Eventually the creature eased into the depths of the blackened forest of Panhandle Trail. We easily classified this as an encounter with Bigfoot.

URBAN LEGENDS

Chase City isn't far from Occoneechee State Park, and it's home to a particularly chilling encounter with the paranormal. Supposedly, a young child in the town died in the 1950s after ingesting a poisonous household liquid. Storytellers say the house is haunted by some variety of specter. Two individuals who spent some time in the house recall a small push toy appearing out of nowhere and seemingly moving with a life of its own, rolling down the hallway with nothing pushing it other than a faint silvery orb.

Another ominous mystery takes place in Clarksville, where a young beauty appears out of thin air and dashes toward vehicles and screams for help. Once near the vehicle, people see that she is not so beautiful after all, as her eyes are sunken and her skin is deathly pale. Wearing a flowing golden gown she pleads for assistance, but when passersby stop their vehicles to assist, the phantom vanishes before their eyes, leaving visitors stunned.

So whether traveling through the park or nearby towns, keep your eyes open and your sixth sense tuned for a glimpse, sound or scent from the beyond.

Sailor's Creek Battlefield State Park

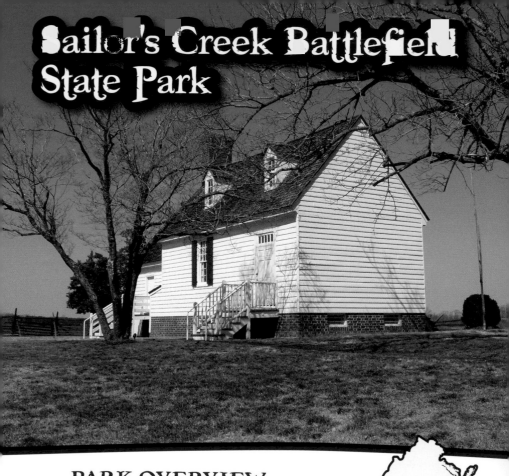

PARK OVERVIEW

ACRES: 370   **FOUNDED:** 1940

NEARBY: Appomattox Court House National Historical Park, Museum of the Confederacy, Sandy River Reservoir, Briery Creek Wildlife Management Area, Lee's Retreat Driving Tour, Moton Museum, Twin Lakes State Park, Holliday Lake State Park, High Bridge Trail State Park

NOTABLE VISITORS: General Robert E. Lee, George C. Custer, Custis Lee

ABOUT THE PARK

Sailor's Creek Battlefield is the site of the Civil War's last major battle. The historic Hillsman House served as a field hospital; it was renovated and reopened in 2009 to reflect the Civil War period. A visitor center was added in 2011 and features a collection of Civil War relics, exhibits and a library with an expansive book and document collection. The park's Confederate Overlook Trail is approximately 1 mile long and has signage interpreting the events of the battle. Monument Trail is very short and takes the visitor to a memorial commemorating those who fought for both armies. Custis Lee Trail was dedicated in Spring 2014 and takes visitors along the perimeter of the historic battle site between Custis Lee's Confederates and Major General Seymour's Federals. Picnic opportunities are available in several locations.

PARK HISTORY

Epicenter of the Final Battle

"My God, has the army dissolved?" pronounced General Robert E. Lee as he overlooked the bloody fields stretching up from Sailor's Creek. He watched in horror as Confederates yielded. Already in retreat from Richmond and Petersburg, Lee's remaining forces ran smack into Union General Philip Sheridan's cavalry and elements of the II and VI Corps at this quiet countryside farm. The date was April 6, 1865—known as Black Thursday among Confederates, as 7,700 young men were captured, injured or killed. The captives included six generals. Robert E. Lee's oldest son, Custis, was among them.

As Ranger Lee Wilcox puts it, if you looked out of the front door of the Hillsman House and across Sailor's Creek Road, "you would have seen part of the fighting that took place at the Hillsman Farmhouse, which was actually the second engagement of the day out of three separate fights that made up the "Battles of Sailor's Creek."

The Hillsman Farmhouse engagement occupied both sides of the road, which was known as the Rice-Deatonville Road in 1865. (Today it is called Saylers Creek Road.) The battle started at the farmhouse, crossed over Sailor's Creek and continued up the opposite bank with both armies still spread out across either side of the road.

Ranger Wilcox provided a map created by the Civil War Preservation Trust that shows how the armies were spread out. From the map, it's clear that the sprawling battles were an act of desperation on the part of the Confederacy; they were simply trying to retreat in order to fight another day.

Miserable conditions prevailed in the days leading up to the battle. Heavy rain began on April 2, and when the battle started, the air was cold and the ground was soaked. Throughout the course of the battle, soldiers found themselves chest high in a cold, swollen creek. Because of the conditions and the carnage, some historians consider this battle the site of the worst fighting in the entirety of the Civil War. Keith Rocco's painting in the Sailor's Creek

Battlefield Visitor Center depicts the horrific hand-to-hand combat that prevailed during much of the fighting.

While the site is known as the battle of Sailor's Creek, there were actually three separate battles that day: the Battle of Hillsman's Farm, the Battle of Marshall's Crossroads (or Harper's Farm), and the Battle of Lockett's Farm (or Double Bridges).

The Hillsman House

The Hillsman House would play an important role in the battle. But the house itself has a long history. It was built in the mid-1700s by Moses Overton, and later inherited by his son, Moses Jr., who was a veteran of the War of 1812. After the war, Moses Jr. returned home to his farmland and built an addition in 1815. Captain Overton raised a family on-site, and his daughter Martha later married John Albert Hillsman. This is how the residence became known as the Hillsman House. However, even today some refer to the home as the Overton-Hillsman House. The house is a fine example of typical dwellings built during the colonial era. It features hand-hewn timbers secured with wooden pegs and anvil-wrought nails. At some point in its history, finely finished plaster walls were added to the interior; both features are sure signs of affluence in the nineteenth century.

Martha and John had a son named James Moses Hillsman who married Lucy Jane Blanton. James enlisted in the Confederate Army and was captured at the Battle of Spotsylvania Courthouse and tossed into a prison camp, while his mother, wife, two children and seven hired hands remained on the property. Up to that point, the property had been untouched by the war, but that was about to change.

The Hillsman House as a Hospital

Once the battle began in earnest, the Hillsman House became a focal point. Perched on a hill, the Hillsman House immediately became a field hospital for both the Union and Confederate troops. The family and servants were quickly rushed to the basement. Upon the first assault across the creek, Lieutenant Peck incurred a slight wound to the hip thus making him one of the first injured to receive treatment at the Hillsman House. Having been treated, Lieutenant Peck is set to the side and records everything he sees. Peck notes that there were two beds in the center room. A wounded officer lay on each bed, with another six wounded officers on the floor. The injured began to overtake the house so the surgeons lined up the patients, leaving only a narrow pathway, in order to hastily continue the surgeries, which often consisted of amputations.

The surgical tools available at the time were crude: saws, probes, sharp blades and retractors. Circular metal bits were used to drill holes into head wounds in an attempt to relieve pressure on the brain. Given the volume of patients, drops of blood soon began hitting the basement floor as it oozed through the floorboard gaps.

The three battles continued throughout the day, leaving dead and wounded bodies scattered across the landscape. When the sun began to set, the fighting subsided. Mrs. Hillsman had had enough. She packed up her mother-in-law, children and hired hands and exited the basement and walked a quarter-mile across the back field to the overseer's home. In the process she walked past multitudes of dead and wounded men. There in the side yard lay a pile of extremities, gruesome horrors to the gentle Hillsman family. Back in those days antibiotics hadn't been discovered, so even minor wounds could end with an amputation. Mrs. Hillsman shuddered in disgust and declared she'd never come back to the house.

One month after the surrender at Appomattox, Mr. Hillsman walked back to his family farm and encountered the remnants of the bloody battle. He quickly learned that his family went to the overseer's home and had since moved elsewhere.

Mr. Hillsman promptly built a new family home next to the overseer's house. Mrs. Hillman later returned, along with her children, and remained on the property until her death in 1917. All three structures remain today; the Hillsman House is open for scheduled tours.

CLAIRVOYANT ENCOUNTERS

While researching this site, I befriended a volunteer at Sailors Creek Battlefield whose husband is a Civil War re-enactor. She also happens to be a medium and was kind enough to tour Hillsman house with me.

Just moments after the medium and I shut the door, we both took deep breaths to relax and center ourselves. The sunshine outside was welcome, yet a chill from the basement air crept into the parlor, and the medium noticed immediately. She tensed her arms and slowly turned in three precise circles as if trying to locate something invisible. Then the medium began to speak: "Mrs. Hillsman used to entertain guests here, but this is also the room where Lieutenant E. Pickett described operating implements dripping with blood after amputations."

We moved from the parlor to the basement. The steps are shallow and steep, the ceiling is low, and the passage is slender at best. Yet we were overwhelmed with curiosity to see where Mrs. Hillsman, her children and her hired servants fled during the battles. As we inched our way down the staircase, the medium led the way telling the author about the basement. It was here where the family members hid and blood from amputated arms, legs and hands dripped between the floorboards, coating them and streaking the walls with blood.

Almost immediately she sensed a spirit, a small child, male perhaps, which hid in the front corner beside the fireplace. She states, "This room is also where a female servant of slight build lingers alongside the side of the fireplace; she proudly tends to the fire, the day's meal, and watches the young lad during her tasks."

The second story of the home consists of two rooms with just a simple entry door dividing the space. The state park staff aren't sure who occupied which rooms—the children or Mrs. Hillsman—but the medium has no such trouble. She recognizes immediately that the room closest to the stairs belonged to the madam and master of the household. She explains, "The headboard faced the staircase, for Mrs. Hillsman's ultimate duty was focused on the well-being of her children. She was a strong guardian." The children had the larger room, which had more space and a long shelf embedded into the wall that adjoined the passageway to another staircase.

In this passageway, which leads to the attic, the medium detected a spirit, that of a child approximately 12–13 years old or perhaps as old as 16, but no older. The staff routinely place a chair in the corridor, and they note that it is found in a different position from time to time. They also occasionally observe a glowing whoosh of an orb speeding through the darkness.

As we left the house and walked on the grounds, Mrs. Lanier continued with a tale from a recent experience. It occurred during a re-enactment, sometime after her husband's unit had set up camp. She walked over to her husband and said, "I didn't know that there were going to be so many re-enactors here." He responded with, "What are you talking about?" Mrs. Lanier pointed across the field beyond the handful of re-enactors and said "Well, all the tents, fire rings with billowing smoke, and even the large number of horses tethered." It was then that he realized she was seeing something he was not.

THE LONE SOLDIER

Another legend has circulated over the years. A young soldier is often seen tending to a cannon outside the Hillsman House. Frequently, he is seen during re-enactments, but he has never been spotted by the medium. Instead, she sees something much more horrific: the many dying soldiers who were placed outside the rear door of the Hillsman House. Historical research corroborates this horrible sight, and in fact, it's well documented that Union soldiers were buried temporarily right outside the rear door. After the formal surrender of General Lee at Appomattox Court House, these Yankees were dug up and taken to Petersburg. The Rebels on the other hand lay decaying and decomposing under the spring sun. Soon after, local residents gathered the bodies and placed them in a mass grave that's location has since been forgotten. As the park manager puts it, "The entire park is hallowed ground."

THE BELOVED BAND

The park is also home to another talked-about ghost tale. It is the tale of a Southern spouse traveling northward to retrieve her husband's body after learning of the horrific engagement at Sailor's Creek. The woman knocks at the Hillsman's door, where she's informed to head over to the overseer's home where Mrs. Hillsman is residing. Reaching the home, she asks for her assistance. Mrs. Hillsman quips that she vowed never to set foot again near that house, but recants when she sees the visibly distraught woman. They search endlessly, and the soaked field now harbors an inescapable stench of death. Eventually, they spot something. With lantern in hand, the young woman gasped when she realized what she saw. A hand—and a shiny golden band, the one she'd offered to her husband just a few short months before. So it was here she found her infant marriage at an end. One has to wonder if this soldier's restless spirit knew of her arrival and reached through the depths to express a final reflection of his eternal love.

OLD ARTIFACTS

When the park was preparing to build its new state-of-the-art visitor center, several individuals were surveying the land, when a park ranger looked down and saw a rifle ramrod sticking straight out of the ground. Amazed, he called the others to come view this piece of history. Today the rifle ramrod is part of the visitor center's exhibits, but one has to ask, how could a simple metal rod less than an inch in diameter survive in the open, upright, for nearly 150 years? Was it just a quirk of history? Or perhaps something supernatural is to blame?

OFFICER EN ROUTE

The park is diligently transforming the park grounds to resemble the conditions present at the time of battle. Much of this work has already been accomplished at and around the Hillsman House, and many workers have reported a strange sight: when standing in the rear yard looking westward to the tree line; look for a cavalryman riding his horse at trees' edge. Many have seen this apparition and describe it as being an officer in full uniform riding westbound, then fading off into thin air as he reaches the ravine.

So whether you're up at the Hillsman House, down along Sailor's Creek, or touring the impressive visitors center, the haunts of this Civil War site are likely to linger for another 150 years on this blood-soaked ground.

Sky Meadows State Park

PARK OVERVIEW

ACRES: 1864   **FOUNDED:** 1975

NEARBY: Appalachian Trail, Graffiti House, Virginia State Arboretum and Experimental Farm

NOTABLE VISITORS: Governor Mills E. Godwin, Paul Mellon, Willard Scott

ABOUT THE PARK

Pastoral and pristine views are a hallmark of Sky Meadows State Park, which attracts nearly 200,000 visitors each year. They venture to the park for its many recreational opportunities, including: hiking access to the Appalachian Trail, primitive individual and group camping, picnicking, and historical tours of the Mount Bleak House. The attractions and amenities are rounded out by a small fishing pond, six miles of equestrian trail and one of Virginia's largest red-headed woodpecker colonies.

PARK HISTORY

The park's beginnings can be traced to Belle Grove, a Federal-style manor house listed on the National Register of Historic Places. It was built by Isaac Settle, who sold the original land tract to his daughter and son-in-law, Betsy and Lewis Edmonds. In turn they sold 148 acres to Isaac's son Abner and wife Mary. During the 1840s, Abner and Mary Settle decided to build a home along the pristine mountain ridge located in the beautiful Shenandoah Valley. The scenery afforded extended views in all directions. The couple decided upon the name for their home— Mount Bleak. "Bleak" had a much different meaning centuries ago; "bleak" was defined as "exposed or breezy." Here they lived comfortably on the land with with their family of 12.

When the Civil War erupted, three of Abner's sons enlisted in the Confederate forces. Isaac Morgan and Abner Carroll joined the independent command of Colonel John S. Mosby, while their brother Thomas Lee, a surgeon, joined the ranks of the 7th Virginia Cavalry. He went on to serve the Cavalries of the 11th, 12th and 13th command during his four years of service. Dr. Thomas Settle played an important role in history in December 1859, as he was the surgeon present for abolitionist John Brown's hanging. It was Thomas who gave the official pronouncement of death before cutting Brown down from the gallows. Strangely, it was Thomas who heard John Brown's grim but accurate prediction, "The sins of this guilty land can only be purged with blood."

Thankfully for the family, all three sons returned home from the war safely. But the four-year conflict had left the family in bad financial shape, so they decided to leave Mount Bleak and move nearby to the village of Delaplane, known at the time as Piedmont Station.

Eventually, British consul general Robert Hadow became enamored with the property in the 1940s. It reminded him of Scotland's Isle of Skye. He found the site perfectly suited for a family summer home and christened it Skye Farm. But it was not until the site became home to U.S. Attorney General John Scott that it became known as Sky Meadows.

Several decades passed and developers soon coveted the location. Luckily, philanthropist Paul Mellon purchased Sky

Meadows in 1973, and the purchase included the Federal-style Mount Bleak House along with 1,132 acres of rolling farmland. Within two years he donated the property for a state park. The Virginia State Parks spent the next several years planning and preparing the new state park, with a grand opening occurring in 1983. By 1987, an additional 248 acres of land was added to the park, along with another 462 acres donated once again by Paul Mellon.

Today, the park boasts a number of features. Among its long list is the farm itself, which is known as the Mt. Bleak-Skye Farm and is recognized as a National Historic District. The site includes 23 buildings with several structures dating between 1780 and 1954. The park also serves as the northernmost entry point to the Appalachian Trail in Virginia. The picturesque Mount Bleak House attracts not only historians but also those interested in paranormal activity.

RESIDENTS REMAIN AT MOUNT BLEAK

Ask folks associated with the park about ghosts, and they are quick to advise you to speak with Park Ranger Budd who has firsthand knowledge of the subject. As a park interpreter, he's well-versed in the park's history, and he's also spent a great deal of time in the park working as a handyman, which is all too often a park interpreter's first job.

Ranger Budd tells of a time when he was working solo in an upper bedroom of Mount Bleak, and he heard the unmistakable sound of footsteps on the hardwood floors. As he proceeded with his repair work, he wondered about the visitor. Knowing the house was not currently open for visitors, he assumed other staff members had caused the noise. Yet the more he thought about it, the more the footsteps sounded unfamiliar; after years of working with someone and hearing them tramp across old wooden floorboards, time and again, you can start to recognize the sound of their footfalls. He didn't recognize any of them, so he decided to say, "Hello, I'm in here." Silence. He thought it strange, but continued working. Again, Ranger Budd heard the muffled footsteps, this time heading up to the third level—a restricted area. At this point, he reckoned it was a park employee. As he proceeded to listen and work simultaneously, the strange shuffling sound descended the slender staircase. Becoming a little miffed, he raised himself from his work and proceeded down the stairs to identify the unresponsive visitor. At the bottom of the staircase, he saw no one. He ventured throughout the first floor, again finding no one. As the building was closed to visitors, the majority of the doors were locked. Budd then proceeded to the unlocked back door where the eighteenth-century stone staircase leads to the rear yard. Once again he found no one. Later, he inquired to the other park staff about the noise, and they informed him no one was even remotely close to Mount Bleak House on that particular afternoon.

Other strange occurrences happen at the Mount Bleak House. During the park's harvest festival, two teenage park volunteers shared their own ghost story. They spoke with a hushed voice, visibly tense. They described the house's layout, paying special attention to the dungeon-like locked closet in one of the bedrooms. When walking by it, they heard muffled footsteps, despite knowing that the closet was securely latched and that all other park staff and volunteers were either outside or on the first floor. They listened closely and heard the faint sounds of someone just on the other side of the door. When they called, "Who's there?" they heard only silence. After reporting this to other workers, they learned that Yankee soldiers were once held captive and imprisoned in this small, bleak space.

GIGGLES IN THE HALLWAY

Finishing up the day's work, Ranger Dave Born decided to stay late at the office. That was a mistake. Not a living soul was in the park that night, except Dave, although there were apparently a few wayward giggling spirits.

Born settled into his office, which was located in the Mount Bleak house adjacent to the dining room. Only the glow from the single bulb of his desk light illuminated the room. All the other rooms and the property grounds were dark. Silence prevailed except for the sound of a few crickets. Never before had the stillness bothered Dave. That is, until he heard something in the hallway. Rising from his desk chair, he recognized the commotion as the sound of children giggling. Opening the door to the hall, no one was there. And after searching throughout the house, he found no children, but perhaps they were there, just invisible, reliving fond memories of a happy past.

CHILDISH ANTICS

Several years back, two young adults came to revisit Mount Bleak. They were the children of a park manager, and Sky Meadows was their father's fortunate assignment, though only one had lived in the house. This tale was told to the park historian as he conducted a tour, thus scaring the daylights out of a few visitors.

The pair had lived in this very beautiful house for a year and a half. It was during their residence that they experienced weird, unexplainable incidents. Apparently furniture would get rearranged while no one was in the house. Disturbing as it was, it was not as spooky as the time they saw a young girl standing in the upstairs bedroom wearing a long, white wispy dress. Surrounded by an overwhelming light, this milky apparition appeared three times, each time to the park manager's daughter.

With numerous sightings occurring over the course of several decades, the park staff believe that the apparition is the ghost of Matilda, a former resident, who some believe resides in the gap between this world and the next.

BELLE GROVE

Historian B. Curtis Chappelear has researched the area's history in detail, and he shares a tale that supposedly occured during the wee hours of the morning in the western section of nearby Belle Grove estate. Apparently within a forested region there is a large rock with a shelf-like protrusion over the top of it; over time the area became known as Titus's Hollow. Titus was a slave who lived near Middleburg, Virginia.

Attempting to escape to freedom, he ended up at this huge granite protrusion and constructed a rough shelter beneath its ledge. Rumors circulated that the old black man died beneath the rock, leaving behind his restless soul.

Allegedly, squirrel hunters prowling the land in the wee hours of the morning will sometimes hear strange noises scurrying past, always heading in the direction of the former slave's shelter.

GRAFFITI HOUSE, JUST A SHORT DRIVE AWAY

The Graffiti House is not far from Sky Meadows; located on the site of the Civil War Battle of Brandy Station, the building makes a wonderful side trip. It's also home to a strange presence that is noticed by humans and animals alike.

Once a field hospital, the Graffiti House now houses many well-preserved Civil War relics and a good deal of information about the battle that took place here. To understand the Graffiti House, it's important to know a little about the battle itself: In June 1863, General Robert E. Lee moved his army north toward Gettysburg. J.E.B. Stuart commanded 9,500 cavalrymen who were designated to protect Lee's infantry. Without warning, 10,000 Union soldiers covertly crossed the Rappahannock River for a surprise attack on the infantry. When the Battle of Brandy Station finally ended, there were 1,400 casualties, and all for naught, as the battle was inconclusive.

While recuperating from battle wounds, soldiers from both sides of the engagement took charcoal and wrote messages on the interior of the Graffiti House. For 130 years these messages were concealed, but during a 1993 renovation, the scribbling was revealed. In 2002, the Brandy Station Foundation purchased the house as a memorial to both sides.

The house and the battlefield are reputedly haunted. One visitor gives a firsthand account of how she heard lullabies being sung in an empty upstairs bedroom. Even the caretaker, Tony Seidita, has a take on the spooky phantoms that live at Graffiti House. He shares a haunting story involving his three cats, which lazily reside at the house. One sunny afternoon, the three felines decided to meander upstairs to enjoy the afternoon sun. Leaning over the counter to make sure I heard every word, he said, "They typically snooze unfazed by the occasional visitor passing in and out of the rooms. But one afternoon while I was tending to paperwork, all three cats raced down the stairs and dashed out the back door . . . as if they'd seen a ghost!"

Visitors are quick to add that they feel a strange pressure upon entering the home. They describe it as a sinking feeling that weighs them down the further into the home they venture.

The day I toured the home, my female boxer dog accompanied me. As we were about to go up the dark back stairs, the dog stared up the stairs and refused to budge. This is very strange for a dog that bounds up and down two staircases each day at home. Leaving the dog behind, I reached the second story to find the famed scribbles on the historic walls. Nothing out of the ordinary happened during the visit, or maybe it did. When I walked in the room, the ceiling fan was not circulating, but when I turned to leave, it was moving. When glancing at the switch, its position was off! Creepy! This was just a sampling of the frights found on this hallowed ground.

Wilderness Road State Park

PARK OVERVIEW

ACRES: 310   **FOUNDED:** 1993

NEARBY: Cumberland Gap National Historical Park, Virginia Heritage Music Trail, Pine Mountain State Park, Natural Tunnel State Park, Southwest Virginia Museum State Park

NOTABLE VISITORS: Daniel Boone, Colonel Joseph Martin, Dr. Thomas Walker, the explorer who named Cumberland Gap

ABOUT THE PARK

Picnicking, trail use and day-touring are the main attractions found at Wilderness Road State Park, but the park offers a wide variety of other amenities. Martin's Station serves as an outdoor living history museum and is the centerpiece of the annual re-enactment of the Raid on Martin's Station. The station is considered one of the most authentically reproduced pioneer forts in the United States. The park also offers tours of the 1870s Karlan Mansion, which is also available for rental. The park's Indian Ridge Trail rewards hikers with scenic mountain views as they follow the route of the original Wilderness Road, and the Wilderness Road Trail takes hikers, bikers and equestrians along a 10-mile trek terminating at Cumberland Gap National Historical Park.

PARK HISTORY

Early Days

The Great Wagon Road, the Bison Trace, the Warriors Path and the Wilderness Road are all names associated with trails used by the area's early inhabitants. After the English colony of Jamestown was established, all of these trails were considered part of the western wilderness. Founded in the mid-1990s, the park includes 10 miles of the original Wilderness Road and is very close to the famous Martin's Station.

Martin's Station

Joseph Martin was the namesake of this pioneer fort. A brigadier general in the Virginia Militia during the Revolutionary War, he lived from 1740 to 1808 and was a close friend of Patrick Henry. Martin's friend Daniel Boone built the Wilderness Road in 1775 soon after the fort was constructed. It was the only station between the start of the Wilderness Road and Crab Orchard (on the edge of the Kentucky settlement) nearly 200 miles away.

In its first 25 years, nearly 300,000 men, women and children traversed the Wilderness Road. The trail passed through the Shenandoah Valley and then through the mountain gaps in Southwest Virginia before eventually leading to the land of milk and honey in the Ohio Valley. Much of the original Wilderness Road is now part of the state highway system.

The principle purpose of Martin's Station was to serve as a safe haven, supply center and resting place for early pioneers. The journey through the gaps was often fraught with difficulties, including American Indian attacks. The Cherokee, Iroquois and Shawnee had lived in the region for thousands of years and their resistance to the settlers did not end until early in the nineteenth century.

The Idea for a Park in Lee County, Virginia

Virginia Delegate Ford Quillen represented the first legislative district of Virginia from 1970–1993. Born in Gate City in 1938, Delegate Quillen had long harbored a dream of creating a state park in Lee County. He envisioned the Karlan Mansion on State Route 58 and its more than 300 acres as the core of a new state park. As his proposed park is only about eight miles from Cumberland Gap, Tennessee, he envisioned that the park could be a gateway to Virginia for travelers coming from Tennessee, Kentucky and Ohio.

One of several sites being turned into a park at the time, the Karlan mansion was originally considered a difficult site to turn into a successful state park, let alone a tourism attraction. However, the Wilderness Road and the Martin's Station history soon became the focus of the park, which highlighted one of America's dynamic periods of exploration and growth. The park's location was nearly perfect to tell this story, and park staff decided that it would house pioneer re-enactors and that a replicated historic fort would be built using information from original journals. Wearing the garb and using the materials and tools available to eighteenth-century pioneers, re-enactors spent several years building the historic fort.

Remarkably, this park is visited by 175,000 people each year and is estimated to have nearly $3 million of annual economic impact on the local area. The re-created Martin's Station is recognized as one of the most authentic pioneer forts in America and is frequently used as a backdrop for historical movies and documentaries.

It's also a popular spot for historical education. Each spring hundreds of re-enactors re-create a raid on the fort by American Indians. The raid depicts the hostilities that had developed between the two cultures. It also highlights the bloodshed shared on both sides during this period of conflict.

A Cultural Crossroads

American Indians have lived in this area for thousands of years, and in the words of C.G. Holland at the University of Virginia, the area served as a "cultural crossroads," because many Indian tribes traveled through the area on the way to or from Cumberland Gap. The same goes for later settlers and colonists.

As a testament to the Indians who lived in the region, there is a historical marker on old SR-58 marking an Indian Mound dating from 1200–1650 AD. Lucien Carr, assistant curator of the Peabody Museum in Boston, led an excavation here in 1877. By proving the connection between this mound and those created by other American Indian groups, Carr refuted the then-popular "lost race" hypothesis, which claimed that a lost race were responsible for building mounds in eastern North America. During the excavation, the mound caved in, killing one researcher and crippling another.

An Ancient Indian Burial Chamber

The park is even home to Cedar Hill Cave, which houses an ancient Indian burial chamber. The cave is approximately 1,400 feet long and complete with skeletons dating from many hundreds of years ago. Sadly, grave robbers and artifact hunters desecrated the graves and have stolen many of the artifacts and cultural resources that could help archaeologists understand the area's early American Indian populations more fully.

Mayhem in the Mountains

The summer season begins early at Wilderness Road, as the re-enactment of the Raid on Martin's Station occurs each May. In the fall—the park's busiest season—park staff are quick to share several folk tales, including several that just may be true.

One of the stories involves an American legend: Daniel Boone. Boone began hunting at the age of 12 when his

father gave him a rifle. Soon Daniel became a skilled hunter and began his long love affair with the wilderness. While volunteering for the British in 1775, Daniel met John Findley, an early explorer of Kentucky. Findley described an area unlike anything Boone had heard of or witnessed. It was described to Boone as a paradise where bison were so mammoth that the ground sunk below their feet. And a land where so many wild turkeys foraged that they all could not fly at the same time. That was enough description for Boone, and he set his mind on exploring the lands to the west.

Boone's closest friend was John Stewart. He was also his companion on hunting expeditions along with being his brother-in-law. At this time American Indian attacks were a real threat. The common practice was for a group of men to splinter; meeting at a destination every two weeks. However, during one such splintered expedition, Stewart encountered a bleak fate, for he never returned. Boone searched for weeks to no avail. It wasn't until five years later that a body was spotted in the hollowed out innards of a sycamore tree. The victim apparently endured a terrible death, for an arrow was still wedged between his shoulder and arm. Beside the body was Stewart's powder horn emblazoned with the initials JS. Alongside the skeletal remains were also those of a decayed dog with a red collar dangling around the fleshless neck bone. Boone recognized both his comrade's powder horn and the collar of his canine companion, Barkley. Apparently, the two were escaping the natives and fled into the cavernous hardwood before being caught.

As modern-day development encroaches almost everywhere, Southwest Virginia remains blessed with remote, off-the-beaten-path opportunities to refresh the soul and replenish the spirit. Yet some who hear the tale about John

Stewart and Barkley refuse to hike near the long-vanished footpath or venture across the nearby open fields in fear of encountering the spirit world and the souls of John and Barkley.

DEATH KNOCKS PREMATURELY

In 1870, Robert and Susan Ely purchased land in the scenic valley near Wilderness Road. The couple were young and dreams were big— perhaps too big. They scrimped and saved eagerly and Robert dreamt of building Susan's perfect home. However, the two were at odds, for Robert not only penciled out sketches of rooms and porches, but he also penciled in the price of materials. Susan, on the other hand, insisted on living in a great mansion and Robert's grumblings went unnoticed.

Susan set her sights on a home adorned with dark walnut trim throughout and lavish Italian marble. Despite their public boasts about the house, Robert felt worried that the house was financially cursed. Others worried the curse was more literal, arguing that the clay that went into the bricks came from sacred ground where his descendants were laid to rest years before.

Not long after the building's bricks were fired, Susan gathered up the children from the drafty structure and boarded a train to Missouri where she would remain until Robert finished the mansion.

For Robert, the days grew long and the heat was intense, slowing construction. Yet Robert's enthusiasm for a timely completion never waned. So on one particularly hot and sticky afternoon, with temperatures reaching one hundred degrees and humidity nearing one hundred percent, Robert decided a short break certainly would not hurt. He ventured down to Indian Creek for an afternoon respite. Refreshed, he went back to working on the mansion until long past dark. The next morning Robert didn't feel quite right. He brushed the lousy feeling aside and plunged headfirst into finishing the mansion. By noon, he knew something was wrong. He sat down, then lay down. One of his helpers felt Robert's head and it was cold and clammy. Fevers were dreaded back in those days, so the helper made a mad dash to the next mountain over, retrieving the nearest doctor. When the doctor arrived at the mansion site, he gathered up Robert and rushed him to a tiny timber cabin. There both Robert and the doctor remained for several days. The fever never broke and the only comfort Robert had on his deathbed was the enjoyment of smoking a cigar.

Unaware of Robert's death, Susan sensed it was time to head back to Southwest Virginia. Filled with excitement to see her new mansion, she decided to pack up the children and purchase train tickets. Still, something seemed awry. After she said goodbye to her Missouri relatives, an uncomfortable tightness settled in the pit of her stomach. The tightness persisted on the eastbound trip to the station in Middlesboro, Kentucky. Here they boarded another train for the last leg of their trip en route to Caylor Depot. Suddenly Susan's "butterflies" turned to dread as she overhead two women speak of a tragic tale of a young man's passing as he awaited his family's return. Gripped with fear, she tried to conceal her fright, but the children soon learned the truth when they disembarked to a tearful gathering of townsfolk.

The beautiful mansion that Robert Ely could not finish was eventually sold to Karl and Ann Harris, who promptly renamed it Karlan Mansion.

But questions about Robert's death linger on. Was his death due to livestock contamination in Indian Creek? Or was the death the result of stress? Whatever the cause, Robert departed this life far too early, or did he? Locals report strange sightings along Wilderness Road, near Martin's Station, and on the lawn of the historic Karlan Mansion. Some say Robert still lurks about, and they claim to hear sounds of hammering and sawing on the grounds. They also claim to smell an occasional waft of a burning cigar drifting across the front porch. But others feel the noises are more like a knocking or rapping and originate with the disturbed souls of early settlers—settlers whose graves were desecrated when the clay bricks were fired. No one knows, but in the words of Sir Isaac Newton, "Energy is not lost or destroyed, it is merely transferred . . ."

York River State Park

PARK OVERVIEW

ACRES: 2,554   **FOUNDED:** 1980

NEARBY: Colonial Williamsburg, Jamestown Settlement, Yorktown Victory Center, Chesapeake Bay National Estuarine Research Reserve, Busch Gardens, Chippokes Plantation State Park

NOTABLE VISITORS: Governors Chuck Robb, Mark Warner, Terry McAuliffe, John Blair, Nathaniel Bacon

ABOUT THE PARK

Daytime Enjoyment

A day-use park with a wide variety of outdoor recreation opportunities, York River State Park covers 2,554 acres of land with 525 acres designated as a Chesapeake Bay National Estuarine Research Reserve. The park also boasts 3.5 miles of breathtakingly beautiful waterfront and 40 miles of trails. Many of the trails are multi-use and have picnic shelters with adjoining playgrounds. The park also has a fishing pond and a 400-foot fishing pier that extends into York River. Without question, this state park is one of the most attractive, pleasurable and "sleeper" daytime destinations on the East Coast. The park is also a fine place to explore the country's early history; the visitor center is home to a number of American Indian and early colonial artifacts.

Historically Significant from the Onset

Traces of 10,000-year-old archaeological sites have been found on the park grounds. Park documents state that there are three significant encampments within its boundaries: an area of Croaker Landing, Fossil Beach and a Paleo-Indian camp located at the ruins of the Henderson House.

The York River

The state park covers a stretch of land between the York River and Interstate 64. The York River, for which the park was named, is formed by the confluence of two rivers at West Point, the Mattaponi on the west and the Pumunkey on the east. Eventually, the York River spills into the Chesapeake Bay, one of the greatest estuaries on the planet. Once referred to by the American Indians as the Great Salt Water, the Bay is between 4 and 40 miles wide and spans a distance of 200 miles, dividing the states of Maryland and Virginia.

The middle of the seventeenth century saw the introduction of English plantations and their accompanying commerce. One of the first was Mount Folly Plantation, located about a mile up from today's park boundary. Records indicate that in 1673, the plantation's holding included 900 acres downstream, including Taskinas Creek, an ideal location for a tobacco wharf and a shipping facility for commodities heading to England.

By the eighteenth century, sizable plantations lined the bountiful waters of York River. Three plantations existed within or just along present-day park boundaries. Perhaps the most significant was Taskinas Plantation, a land holding of 1,500 acres, owned by John Blair Jr., one of the forty signers of the U.S. Constitution. Blair, a member of the First Families of Virginia, was also one of the first justices of the U.S. Supreme Court in 1789 and was appointed by George Washington. However, he resigned his position in 1796 and died at the age of 68. The plantation passed to his son-in-law, Reverend James Henderson, who built Henderson House, a brick colonial structure. The quaint but efficient structure was erected in 1817, just footsteps from the York River and today's Fossil Beach.

The Civil War

Because of the prominent geographic location, the park was heavily involved in the Civil War. The Riverview Plantation is thought to have served as a Union Army hospital during the 1862 Peninsula Campaign. When the Civil War finally came to a close on May 9, 1865, the South was left in ruins. Southerners changed their labor-intensive tobacco plantations into smaller grain-producing farms in an effort to survive and recuperate financially.

The land that would become York River State Park passed through many hands, and by the twentieth century, what was once a portion of the Riverview Plantation just south of Taskinas Creek fell under the ownership of a Mr. William

H. Richards. "Old Richards," as he was known, built a respectable home that would factor in a number of future stories at the park.

Demolition at the Park

A state park is always a work in progress. This was certainly the case back in 1975 when the York River staff demolished many abandoned structures at the park, including a number of homes that were viewed as old or insignificant or that were overrun by wildlife and being reclaimed by nature. After the structures were razed, debris was then gathered in a large heap and burned so that nothing remained. That was the plan, at least.

WITCHES AND TEENS

Old Richards House, accidentally called "Richardson's" on an 1863 map due to the mapmaker's mistake, was actually the two-story house of Old Richards. The rambling wreck was constructed by men with apparently little skill, for the house always looked ready to tumble over at the slightest gust of wind. Mr. Richards intended to fix this, so he had laborers lodge large brick pillars beneath the front eaves. Despite its face-lift, the structure always harbored an ominous, ramshackle appearance.

The Old Richards House was built somewhere between 1856 and 1862, and by the mid-1930s it was so dilapidated that what remained was just a shell of a home. The abandoned weather-worn house with its broken out windows, gangly shrubbery and lopsided pillars caught the attention of local teenagers who thought it must certainly be haunted. It became a place for a rite of passage among local teenagers. Rumor was that they were "tested" by spending one night alone within the creepy corridors before being fully accepted into the local ranks. Rumors of incantations and visions of shadowy witch dances kept most teens at bay.

When the Commonwealth purchased the land and structure, they set about demolishing it. Before it could be razed, staff needed to acquire clearance from park officials, so the home remained standing for some time. A large sign that read "Trespassers Keep Out" was draped over the doorway in the hopes of warding off teenaged thrill-seekers.

One off-duty park staffer made an unplanned visit to the Richards House while on a hike. With his dog at his side, he made his way through the deep coastal forest. Without warning, a blast of cold wind descended from the western sky and the sky turned to a morbid gray. A formidable squall was racing towards him. Soon, lightning and thunder crashed and boomed and the trees whipped back and forth in the wind.

Along with his dog, he sprinted toward the closest shelter, the Richards House. Leaping onto the rickety porch, the two felt a bit of slight relief when all of a sudden the house seemed to be ablaze. The strange thing was, there was no heat from the flames. Spooked out of its wits, the dog broke loose and tore into the darkness. Terrified, the staff member dashed after his dog, and within minutes both were safely home, but still reeling from the surreal experience. He never returned to the Richards House until accompanied by a bulldozer and other staff members, under the brightness of a noonday sun.

Today, the Old Richards House lives on in memory and in legends that are shared on the park's "Ghost Trails" ride, a hayride held each October.

THE BLACK WIDOW OF WOODSTOCK POND

Woodstock Pond is a tranquil bit of the park, but it was once the site of a haunting tragedy. The year was 1957, and locals James and Eleanor decided to exchange vows on the shores of the pond. Each grew up nearby, and they had spent many an afternoon in the park. When James proposed to Eleanor, she knew exactly where and when the two would exchange vows—Woodstock Pond. One of their favorite childhood memories was lying in the lush green grass gazing up to the heavens with its thousands of glistening stars. Eleanor decided an evening ceremony was best. The happy event soon arrived, and strangely, not many on the invitation list came.

The dim, glow of the flickering torchlights that lit the scene almost seemed to foretell gloom. The proceedings were short and sweet and no one could predict what would happen next. Not even the two who had planned it!

Just after the preacher said, "You may now kiss the bride," their longtime friends, the Best Man and Maid of Honor, suddenly grabbed the groom and threw him into the water. This was a joke they had planned ever since they found that the wedding was going to be held at Woodstock Pond. The prank seemed innocent enough, but no one could have foreseen the tragedy that followed.

When grabbing the groom, he put up a struggle. The pier was now slick from the evening dew and all three laughingly tumbled into the water. But as James plunged headfirst, he hit a rock, breaking his neck and killing him instantly. In the dimly lit setting, no one noticed he hadn't come back up. When they finally did realize it, they discovered his lifeless body. James had drowned in the shallows of Woodstock Pond.

Horrified at what just happened, Eleanor wailed aloud. Instantly, those in attendance fell from bouts of laughter to pools of tears. Eleanor gathered her composure, then hissed at the Best Man and the Maid of Honor, vowing that James' early death would curse them.

The curse was apparently real, because the couple disappeared. Weddings promptly ceased at Woodstock Pond, for soon after their disappearance it was thought that the dead souls of the Best Man and Maid of Honor lurked below the shadowy waters, waiting to grab the next groom.

PHANTOMS AT MOODY'S WHARF

Taskinas Plantation was a colonial tobacco plantation for about 100 years. Today, its brick ruins are tucked away at the intersection of Spur and Powhatan Forks Trails. It played an integral role in the colonial era, and many relics from the period are found here by archaeologists. Because water traffic was essential in the early history of the area, many of the park's trails were once the original pathways to what was known as Moody's Wharf. Here the colonists established one of many inspection and packing wharfs where their products waited for the next tall ship to carry them back to England

and beyond. Tobacco was grown here for so long that even today you can make out some of the old planting furrows off of Mattaponi trail; the trail that leads to Moody's Wharf is a short distance down from what is now known as Fossil Beach.

What led to the downfall of Moody's Wharf? After some careful digging, archaeologists have been able to shed light on a few incidents that could have led to its demise. It seems the year was 1720 when two industrious young businessmen, one named Elijah and the other Jonathan, acquired Moody's Wharf. Initially, their venture was very profitable, but as profits were booming, Jonathan started to notice some strange happenings around the wharf. The original workers were replaced with shadier characters. Jonathan quickly took the matter into his own hands and decided to investigate for himself. He soon spotted an unmarked ship loading barrels of cargo late one moonless night. In a flash, Jonathan knew these unscrupulous men were stealing from the wharf, but he mistakenly cast blame on the hands of his business partner, Elijah. Racing to Elijah's home with his temper raised, he confronted him. Elijah was so enraged that he hastily challenged Jonathan to a duel along the banks of the wharf the very next morning. Outraged, Jonathan agreed. With swords, the two fought on the docks of Moody's Wharf. Little did Jonathan know, his skills as a swordsman were no match for Elijah's, as Elijah had served as a captain on an English privateer vessel—a pirate ship.

It's not clear who won the duel, but both disappeared afterwards. No bodies were ever found and Moody's Wharf soon burnt to ruins. Some say the outcome was not decided and the duel still goes on to this day. Reports emerge from time to time about two faint apparitions that still appear to be fighting with old-fashioned swords.

JUST DOWN RIVER

Just down the river and across the brackish waters of
the York lies one of America's most historic sites. Its name
is Werowocomoco, an Algonquian phrase meaning "a place
where houses are built." Why a place where houses are
built? Well, archaeologists have discovered that back in the
seventeenth century this site was a major fortress for Chief
Powhatan, leader of the Powhatan Confederacy. It was home
to approximately 9,000 braves and their families. But it was
more than that. It was also the center of their government,
served as a trading post, and so much more. This village was
vibrant, and Englishmen were surprised to discover such a
highly developed society in the area. The colonists, including
John Smith, were inspired by their sophistication, dignity and
societal accomplishments. Archaeologists have since discovered
a ditch surrounding this village that consisted of sacred ground
and is filled with artifacts thousands of years old.

Chief Powhatan's home was a longhouse and also his
courtroom. It is there, within the bark-lined walls of the
longhouse, that John Smith was reputedly faced with
execution in the year 1607. According to legend, Powhatan's
favorite daughter, Pocahontas, threw herself over his body
pleading for the Englishman's life. Her father assented, only
to have her kidnapped by the colonists six years later. It was
during her captivity, in the year 1614, that she married local
settler and tobacco farmer John Rolfe. She bore him a son in
1615, and the three headed to England in 1617, where she died
a short time later.

Hopefully, Werowocomoco will become one of America's
newest national parks. Creating a national park takes a great
deal of effort and planning. It also occasionally turns up some
ghost stories.

My husband and I were invited to visit the site—which is
on sacred ground—and after discussing the site's history and

its geography, the owners mentioned a ghostly encounter with a fawn.

As the story goes, the owners, a married couple, very much enjoyed gardening. One afternoon the wife decided to retreat to her favorite garden spot and lie down for a nap. While napping she felt a gentle nudge at her nose. She slowly opened her eyes and found herself face-to-face with a young fawn. Its large dark eyes and snow-white spots told her it was only a few weeks old. Neither was afraid, and over time, the fawn became a fixture in the garden, almost like a domesticated animal. She came to call it "the little one." Often the fawn would sit at her side and even place its head in her lap. Years later archaeologists were doing a dig at their property directly on the spot of this special garden. At this exact location, the remains of a young female were interred. When an American Indian chief was invited to perform a ceremonial rite over the interred remains, he held an eagle feather in one hand and a smoking sage wand in the other as he lifted his arms and face skyward, asking the gods to bless "the little one." Coincidence? Perhaps not.

GHOST ON THE PENINSULA

Soon after we heard that story, the man of the house led my husband Joe down to the peninsula's edge, where he proceeded to share another ghost story associated with the land.

On a farm or a ranch, repairing fences is a continual task and hired hands can be very useful. This is why on occasion he'd hired two men to assist him while working. On one early morning, as the fog was gently rolling across both the water and landscape, the three men found themselves short of the proper tools. The owner headed back up to the barn, leaving the two hired hands to continue working. Minutes later the landowner returned to find both men mumbling, with glazed eyes and in a trance-like state. When he asked what happened, they reported that they had seen a figure walking across the watery marsh. Trying to puzzle it over, they surmised that it was just a homeless vagrant who got sidetracked in the early morning fog.

As a stubborn foggy mist remained clinging to the landscape, the owner walked down to the edge of the creek, and along with the hired help, he watched the figure of a man walk out across the creek. Thinking they'd misjudged the creek's edge because of the fog, they all took several steps forward only to realize their eyes weren't playing tricks on them; the man literally floated out across the water. Within a moment, this magical being seemed to evaporate, as the dawn's early light sliced through the fog.

With a quiet shaky voice, one man mustered enough strength to whisper the words of St. James, "for you are a mist that appears for a little time and then vanishes."

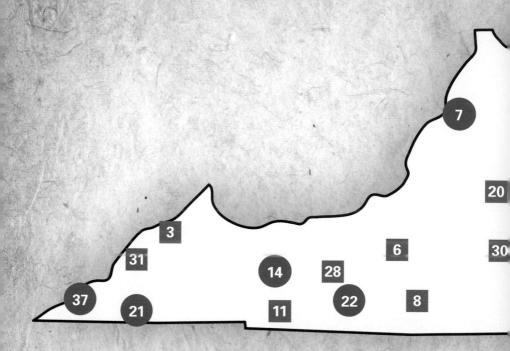

Featured Virginia State Parks

Other Virginia State Parks

VIRGINIA STATE PARKS

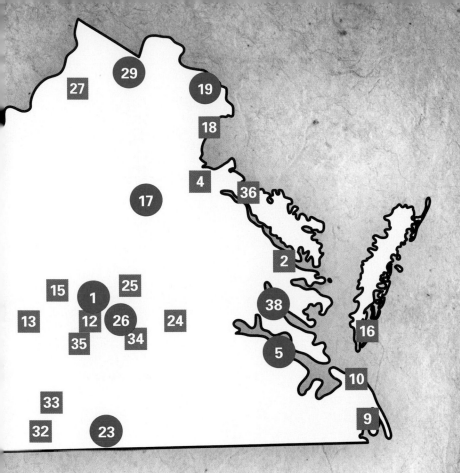

21 Natural Tunnel

22 New River Trail

23 Occoneechee

24 Pocahontas

25 Powhatan

26 Sailor's Creek Battlefield

27 Shenandoah River

28 Shot Tower

29 Sky Meadows

30 Smith Mountain Lake

31 Southwest Virginia Museum Historical

32 Staunton River

33 Staunton River Battlefield

34 Tabb Monument

35 Twin Lakes

36 Westmoreland

37 Wilderness Road

38 York River

ABOUT THE AUTHOR

Patricia Marsh Elton was born in Cincinnati, Ohio, and educated in Ohio schools before attending Hocking College and Ohio State University. She is a resident of Powhatan, Virginia. Her writing career began with Wildernet.com as an outdoors writer in 1999. Patricia is a master naturalist, avid birder and lover of the outdoors. Her copy and photographs have introduced thousands to the majesty of our nation's state and federal public lands. Patricia's fascination with the spirit world and her first ghostly encounter began during her high school days while living on a small farm in central Ohio. Her husband Joe served as Virginia's state parks director for twenty years, and it was during this period that she became intimately familiar with Virginia's state parks and the rich oral and written history associated with these places. The Eltons have two adult sons.